INTERIOR DESIGN FOR SMALL DWELLINGS

Interior Design for Small Dwellings addresses the onrush of interest in smaller homes and the possibility that small dwellings might be the answer to housing needs and sustainability. The book explores key principles essential to residing and designing small interiors with emphasis on client involvement and implementation of participatory, inclusive design as advocated by the Council for Interior Design Accreditation.

Does living in a small space mean living small? The authors believe that by simplifying one's life intelligently and applying certain principles of design, planning and organization, one can actually live a meaningful life in a smaller space. These tenets are based on the authors' professional experiences and living in small homes. To this end, the book provides discussion, images, case studies, interviews, worksheets, activities and suggested explorations.

Interior Design for Small Dwellings is a teaching guide and provides information and exercises that help professional designers utilize design theory, space planning and programming techniques. Throughout, the text affords sustainability, biophilic design and wellness methodologies. It is also a practical manual offering designers and, ultimately, clients design tips for

- **storage space**
- **small kitchen design**
- **multifunctional, flexible furnishings, fixtures and equipment**
- **recycling methods**
- **entertaining in small spaces**

Importantly, the book offers a **St. Helena Library** meeting the personal needs of individuals and the power of sim 1492 Library Lane es and dwellings we recognize what is important to us and validat St. Helena, CA 94574 contributes to not only sustainability, but to connectivity with nature **(707) 963-5244** ok will assist the professional designer to impart these idea

Sherrill Baldwin Halbe, PhD, is a professional interior designer and instructor of interior design at San Francisco State University and Montana State University's Gallatin College and School of Architecture. Dr. Baldwin Halbe has taught interior design for two decades and has presented and published interior work nationally. With first-hand experience of living in a 600 square feet home in the Napa Valley, California, her theoretical background, design experience and aesthetic sensibilities provide understanding of living smaller and simpler.

Rose K. Mark, MA, is an educator, learning specialist, writer and food professional. Her food and travel articles have been published internationally. Her personal journey, planning a 624 square feet home, in addition to inhabiting a number of diverse small dwellings, have given her insight and lessons on how living smaller and simpler can provide a richer lifestyle.

INTERIOR DESIGN FOR SMALL DWELLINGS

SHERRILL BALDWIN HALBE AND ROSE K. MARK

Routledge
Taylor & Francis Group

NEW YORK AND LONDON

First published 2019
by Routledge
711 Third Avenue, New York, NY 10017

and by Routledge
2 Park Square, Milton Park, Abingdon, Oxon, OX14 4RN

Routledge is an imprint of the Taylor & Francis Group, an informa business

© 2019 Taylor & Francis

The right of Sherrill Baldwin Halbe and Rose K. Mark to be identified
as authors of this work has been asserted by them in accordance with
sections 77 and 78 of the Copyright, Designs and Patents Act 1988.

Library of Congress Cataloging-in-Publication Data
A catalog record for this title has been requested

ISBN: 978-1-138-58363-4 (hbk)
ISBN: 978-1-138-58365-8 (pbk)
ISBN: 978-0-429-50660-4 (ebk)

Typeset in Akzidenz Grotesk and Franklin Gothic
by Out of House Publishing

Rose:
To Larry,
Who built a home within my heart

Sherrill:
To Steve
With love and thanks

CONTENTS

PART 2

DESIGN CONSIDERATIONS

ACKNOWLEDGMENTS

Rose:

This book was inspired by my co-author, Sherrill Halbe. Each visit to her small home opened my eyes to how efficient and creative use of space and materials allowed her to live with less material goods, thereby opening up room in her life for more meaningful experiences.

I am indebted to my friends who graciously shared their home for photographs, inspiration, as well as tips on living well in small spaces. Special thanks to Elaine Maute, Daniel Weber, Cathy Nyhan, Saddhana Seelam, Jorge Freyer, Andy Blasky, Elizabeth Chafcouloff and Jyoti Rae for sharing their homes and interior life with me. I am forever grateful to Christian Zimmerman and his brother Jeff Zimmerman for developing and building Phoenix Commons, the best and smallest home I have ever lived in.

Sherrill:

Many thanks to Rose for her friendship and her enthusiasm, intelligence and dedication in spreading the word about living well in small dwellings.

We sincerely thank Katharine Maller, Architecture Editor at Routledge, Taylor and Francis for their assistance and for making it happen.

I'd like to extend special thanks to all of my family, friends, students and colleagues for a wealth of insight, help and support. To all of our contributors who shared their homes, ventures and designs; to our readers, photographers and computer experts who saved the day; and my family who smartly and patiently listened, encouraged and contributed – I thank you.

SMALLER, SIMPLER DWELLINGS: DESIGNING A MEANINGFUL LIFE

DOES LIVING IN A SMALL SPACE MEAN LIVING SMALL?

Figure 0a.1. Living big in a small dwelling.

Source: Michael Hospelt Photography, WEISBACH architecture | design, Gar Rector and Associates.

We don't think so. We are convinced that people can hold onto things that have meaning while letting go of the excess that complicates their lives. Through conscious planning, thoughtful use of materials and some soul-searching one can achieve a rewarding intentional life, even in a small dwelling.

If you are one of the many professionals who face the challenge of designing for clients who want to live in a small home, we offer this book as a guide to use with your clients. We also submit this book as a teaching benchmark, a practical manual and a philosophy

based on meeting individual personal needs and the power of simplicity. We contend that by simplifying our lives and dwellings we
can recognize what is important to us and validate who we are. It
is our belief and objective that living simply contributes to not only
sustainability, but to connectivity with nature and other people. Our
book will help you impart these ideals.

In addition, as the ever-evolving design profession is shifting to participatory, inclusive design, advocated by the Council for Interior
Design Accreditation (CIDA) Professional Standards, 2017, this
book will help you comply and embrace these opportunities and
responsibilities. We will guide you and your client through every step
of the process.

We have the information here for you when you need it. Programming
exercises, including worksheets, are provided to help you and your
client identify the client's unique design issues and solutions. We
offer a complete sample of a design program, with a client interview,
to give examples of what you might experience when codesigning
with clients.

Armed with knowing what your client wants, we will help you develop
their space and design. We will show you how to choose colors and
finishes that complement a smaller area and at the same time satisfy
their dreams and desires.

As you design the client's dwelling to fit their needs and desires, we
offer you and your client some specific, practical strategies for successfully living small. You'll learn how to guide your client in opening
up more space and show how to identify unnoticed potential space.
We provide information on how to use professional interior design
methodology in new and participatory ways. We deliver innovative
strategies about how to use multifunctionality, flexibility and adjustability tactics. We share with you the beauty and value of recycled
items and tell where you can find them. We recall tips that earlier
generations and other cultures have used to save money and space.

Lastly, we show you how entertaining in small spaces is possible with basic strategies and approaches for parties of every size.

We have seen amazing and exciting examples of small interiors. Not only the homes of wealthy individuals, but of folks with modest incomes who have creatively furnished and designed their homes. We share their design strategies, images and comments throughout the book. Their stories will inspire and assist you to use inventive and affordable means to design a home that expresses individual personality and preferences.

HOW WE GOT HOOKED: OUR PERSONAL STORIES

Sherrill
Rosehaven Cottage

I live small. I initially built my pied-à-terre for a vacation rental, happily situated in the wine region of the Napa Valley in California. I also designed the cottage with the following objectives in mind.

- **To restore the 1930s 600 square feet (55.74 square meters) cabin and save it from deterioration while retaining its "footprint." Increasing the square footage would have been prohibitive.**
- **To profit from the weekend rental.**
- **To enjoy the life of a "snowbird" in my later years – living seasonally in both Montana and California.**
- **To live sustainably.**

I built small because of the physical restraints imposed by the land and county building codes. But, I must say, as a designer, I liked the challenge of creating a space that would meet my physical, emotional and aesthetic needs within these constraints. Also, by using

Figure 0a.2. Kitchen area in Rosehaven Cottage in the Napa Valley.

Source: Sherrill Baldwin Halbe Interior Design; Mark Lund Photography, Gar Rector and Associates.

the existing footprint I was able to manage the cost of constructing a tiny house, which not only gave me a rental property but equity in a second home.

My first goals were to design for functionality, flexibility and adjust-ability. I wanted rental practicality with vacation comfort and pizzazz. Within this tiny space, I created a living room, kitchen, bedroom, bathroom and laundry room. I did this by establishing multiple-use designs that gave the illusion of spaciousness. At the same time, my

Figure 0a.3. The deck is like living in a tree house.

Source: Sherrill Baldwin Halbe Interior Design; Mark Lund Photography, Gar Rector and Associates.

design reflected the Napa Valley's natural environs of vineyards, rich soil, flowers and sun patterns.

Because I built the cottage on the top and the edge of a hillside, surrounded by oak trees, I wanted to evoke the wondrous feeling of living in a tree house.

I had a deck built around the cottage and cut out a space for an existing tree to continue its growth from below the deck. The cottage has an indoor–outdoor ambiance, overlooking the wooded area and garden below.

Now that I live in the cottage part of the year, I experience an interior that has an airy feel with lots of natural light and splendid views through French doors, windows and a skylight. I was influenced by the Napa Valley earth tones and foliage in my choice of interior finishes and colors. I chose a wonderful paint color, Burlesque, that is a subtle, slight beige, peach and white combination. This soft and creamy color tends to shift with the changing light of day and creates different depths of color on each wall and ceiling plane.

Vaulted ceilings, rounded wall corners, curved cabinetry and staggered tile work allow the eye to endlessly explore the interior space without feeling uncomfortably enclosed.

The L-shaped step-in tile shower/bath, with a foot fountain and a window, makes the minuscule bathroom feel roomy and luxurious.

Less is more in this design at Rosehaven Cottage, providing me a sense of place and a "foot on the ground." My home has made me aware of the importance and value of smaller living and attentive to the strategies others are taking to achieve this end.

Rose
A Journey of Discovery

During my life I have lived in numerous dwellings, four of which I owned. In none of those places was I able to feel an emotional connection to my home. I consulted books on design and color, I read loads of magazines, I tore out pages that captured a sense of what I wanted, but I couldn't put it all together. I could never put my finger on how other people were able to capture their personality in their homes.

When I retired, my husband and I decided to sell our 1600 square feet (148.65 square meters) house and downsize for various

Figure 0a.4. Vaulted ceilings allow the eye to explore the space without feeling enclosed.

Source: Sherrill Baldwin Halbe Interior Design; S. Gannon, Gar Rector and Associates.

reasons. Our plan was to move, sell the house first and house-sit for friends and family during our search for our new home.

By sheer luck and great timing we found out about Phoenix Commons, a cohousing community development for active 55 plus folks that was being built within walking distance to an area where we had always wanted to live. We found several small condominium units within our price range. Our unit would be only 624 square feet (57.97 square meters), but we would have access to a number of communal rooms where we could cook and dine with the other residents as well as engage in other community activities. We opted

Figure 0a.5. A step-in tile shower doubles for bathing.

Source: Sherrill Baldwin Halbe Interior Design; Mark Lund Photography, Gar Rector and Associates.

for less private space in exchange for the opportunity to improve the quality of our living circumstances.

Would we be able to pull it off? Could we live in this much reduced space? I had only to look at how Sherrill and her husband did this in their 600 square feet (55.74 square meters) home to see that it was indeed possible.

As this would be our *last home* I really wanted to make sure that it reflected the heart and spirit of my husband and me. What was the theme of our lives; what was important to us. At the same time it had to be as functional as possible in order for us to continue our work as writers and do the things we loved such as cooking and entertaining.

This is when Sherrill stepped in to help. She conducted an interview with me to explore how I envisioned my dream home and walked me through a series of steps and exercises at that time.

Sherrill asked me to list every room I would have in my new home and include everything that was needed there. What colors, textures and objects would I have in it? What emotion did I want to experience in each room? We went down checklists of room sizes, dimensions of cabinets, storage spaces and appliances. She explained to me that good design was a holistic combination of form and function. She wanted me to list what would be in each room, but also to consider the function of each object.

I have always been a very practical person; never allowing myself to voice my desires. I worried that I would make mistakes, waste money or seem foolish to others. Now in answer to Sherrill's questions I hesitantly said that I had always dreamt about having a living room wall painted a Moroccan red. Immediately I backed down and said, "Oh, that couldn't work in such a small space."

Sherrill assured me that it could indeed work if we planned the other elements in the room with care. I felt light and giddy. I started imagining all the other colors I had always wanted but had denied myself. I gave myself permission to go on imagining because here was an expert telling me my visions weren't foolish or impractical.

Sherrill's programming exercises helped me focus on what I had, what was important to me, and what I no longer needed. With each exercise I gained greater clarity of what I held close to my heart. At the same time, the functional aspect of the task list grounded me in what I actually had to work with. These tools were the things that had been missing from all the books and magazines I had read.

As I discovered what was meaningful for me I started to form a connection to my possession and through them I gained insights into what I really wanted in my home.

My home is a work in process and progress. I feel it reflects my husband and me because I took part in designing our interior with the help of my designer friend, Sherrill. I want to share this powerful experience with others as they step forward in designing their home with the help of their designer.

Rose and Sherrill

We have become acutely aware of the importance and value of smaller living. We know the worth of a simpler, sustainable lifestyle. Through our collective experiences of being codesigners, educators and small dwelling homeowners we present strategies that will help designers and clients work together in designing small dwellings and a meaningful life.

REFERENCES

Council for Interior Design Accreditation Professional Standards. 2016. "Professional Standards 2017." https://accredit-id.org/wp-content/uploads/2017/01/II.-Professional-Standards-2017.pdf.

AN ARGUMENT FOR SMALLER, SIMPLER, SUSTAINABLE LIVING

Why care about smaller, simpler and sustainable living? We care because we want to satisfy clients' personal needs and values. We care because we want to live a healthier, more meaningful life on this planet we call Earth.

The movement for sustainability is fueled by a growing awareness that we live on a fragile, limited planet. Many of the natural resources we need for survival are running out. We must find ways we can continue to live comfortably while supporting the Earth's health.

Interior Design for Small Dwellings helps one create a thoughtful life by designing home interiors using sustainable approaches. It sets forth methods for managing a household using less money, time and energy.

As individuals we need to make conscious choices about what we purchase and use. We need to choose products made of materials that are not in danger of depletion and are renewable or recyclable. We need to consume less in our daily lives and cut down on waste.

Is living with less the same as deprivation? Not at all. How often we hear people say, "I wish my life were simpler." In many ways, living smaller and simpler is more rewarding than living large and complicated. Sitting on a bench in nature or a comfortable chair; one perfectly ripe peach or a slice of really good bread are simple but sublime experiences. Sharing a cup of tea, sipping a bowl of soup with a friend, or hosting a dinner party where there is lively exchange of thoughts and ideas can be as satisfying as the meal partaken.

This book will show your clients and you how to live with less while gaining more pleasure in life. It is entirely within one's reach to create a more meaningful life when recognizing the important elements that bring happiness and satisfaction to an individual. When an individual focuses on what she has and its function, she can distinguish and clarify what is important. The ability to see clearly allows deep inner needs to come forth. The book will help your client:

- **Personalize the interior of one's dwelling**
- **Discover what is important in one's life**
- **Gain a greater sense of connection to nature and community**
- **Recognize and savor the myriad of simple pleasures that are available**
- **Waste less money**
- **Gain more buying power**
- **Save time and energy in the kitchen**
- **Entertain with less stress and more fun**

A well-designed home can provide a refuge from the stress one encounters in the world. Creating an environment that enhances one's inner life can be a challenge for many. Our book provides the tools to create such a place.

PLAN OF THE BOOK

Participatory design is a major theme of the three part book. In Part 1, we help you analyze client needs and apply simple planning techniques. Part 2 discusses design theory considerations that you can use when designing a small place. In Part 3 we offer practical solutions for specific design problems when living small. The structure of the book allows you to skip around and read whatever interests you at the time or sequentially as you embark on learning how one can live a smaller, simpler and richer life. This book can also be shared with clients so that you can work together as a team in the design process. Most chapters include case studies, sample worksheets, activities and suggested explorations.

The resource section includes 22 exercise worksheets based on the text information in Parts 1, 2 and 3. Both the designer and client can use the worksheets. This section also includes a program template with a checklist and Excel spreadsheets for keeping track of records. We've also included a sample program.

Part 1 consists of three chapters. The first two chapters present discussion and an exercise in Chapter 2 to help process and focus on what is important to the client in designing a particular small space. The next chapter looks at programming: a look at what is needed in the design, what already exists, budget and future needs. We present participatory and codesign programming exercises to support the understanding of essential needs. These exercises will help designers and their clients ascertain personal considerations in designing small homes. Discussion, exercises and worksheets cover programming and include: daily routines; inventory of furnishings and accessories; essential, desired and future needs; physical interior characteristics; building in context; functional need in different rooms; aesthetic needs; environmental needs for universal, accessible, aging in place and healthy design; and discussion with a budget and scheduling exercise to help estimate projects.

Case Study 1 looks at cohousing where residents own their individual, small condominiums. We've included an interview with Rose, who designed the interior of her small dwelling in Case Study 2. Case Study 3 looks at a small house built specifically for health and well-being.

Part 2 discusses design considerations. Chapter 4 provides an overview of the importance of design and the design process. Then Chapter 5 describes designing a space with elements and principles of design – with small in mind. We discuss color and light and specifically present ways designers and clients can use color and light to their advantage. Chapter 6 advocates participatory and inclusive objectives as it explores color preferences; color guidelines; psycho-logical, sociological and cultural aspects of color; physical consider-ations; color schemes; and tips from color experts. These chapters include exercises for both client and designer in learning to see color and to identify preferences.

Case studies exemplify design theory and cultural considerations. Case Study 4 illustrates development of a shipping vessel's living space design, which required solutions to issues ranging from safety compliances to cultural dynamics. Case Study 5 presents a narrative on how a program and design theory revealed solutions for a small multiuse home. Case Study 6 shows the process of getting the color right for a young couple's bedroom.

In Chapter 7 we discuss small dwelling design development, detailing, space planning and design theory based on codesign programming evidence. We present multifunctional, flexible and adjustable attributes throughout. Topics include space planning: how to put it all together and designing Rose's condo. Here we have included checklists and suggested explorations. The theme, "designing for Rose's condominium," runs throughout the book from beginning to end. Case Study 7 exemplifies these principles.

Chapter 8 presents ways to tap into nature and sustainability with the following topics: nature, biophilia and interior design; nature's inspiration and well-being; sustainability and responsibility; and how to implement sustainable principles. A case study describes remodeling a bathroom sustainably. We share designer and client examples, exercises and images.

Part 3 offers five chapters on specific problem areas when designing small. *Finding More Storage* describes ways to find space using a non-linear approach. *The Small Kitchen* shows ways to save time, energy and money in this crucial workroom and includes a kitchen remodel case study.

Chapter 11 offers multifunctional, flexible and adjustable furnishing, fixtures and equipment ideas. Chapter 12 provides resources on how and where you can find and use recycled items. We also discuss the concept of recycled knowledge from past generations and other cultures, which are both sustainable and practical. We have included a case study describing a collectible and antique shop in Sonoma, California, which features past and global pieces.

Chapter 13, *Let Me Entertain You*, is replete with strategies and approaches for entertaining intimate and large parties in small quarters. We cover common problems and suggestions when entertaining and present design solutions. We have included examples of different settings and showcase *The Power of Interior Design for Small Dwelling Entertainment: Libby Design Associates' Innovative Design Solution for a Dining Room.*

Part 1

ANALYZING YOUR CLIENTS' NEEDS

Chapters 1–3

CHAPTER 1

WHY SMALL LIVING AND FOR WHOM

Figure 1.1. This living room reflects the client's personal characteristics, values and attitudes.

Source: Hole Photography, B. and H. Hartsock, Gar Rector and Associates.

OVERVIEW: WHY SMALL LIVING AND FOR WHOM

This chapter looks at various personal characteristics, values and attitudes and discusses who might benefit from living in a small residence. Your client might be one of the following individuals who want a simpler life while enriching their domesticity with fewer resources. Your clients may:

> Have concerns about economics and value quality with less consumption
> Want to live in a preferred area but cannot afford to live there unless they live in a smaller home
> Care about living lighter on the Earth
> Value simplicity and mindfulness

The concept that big and expensive belongings equate value is being replaced with an appreciation for things that are small, simple and well made. Easy, uncomplicated approaches for everyday living are being sought in response to the complex demands of life in a continually changing technological world.

People in every demographic, from young adults just starting out to retiring baby boomers, are choosing smaller, more affordable dwellings in order to live in prime locations. Proximity to one's workplace, support services and areas that hold special interest such as good schools, shops and entertainment are major factors that influence a person's choice of location. Equally important is the ability to afford housing in these prime areas. How can a person with a modest income afford a dwelling that meets their needs? For many, the answer is living in a smaller home.

From the outset, "small dwelling" begs to be defined. Some say that a tiny house is between 60 and 400 square feet (5.57 and 37.16 square meters) and a small house is larger. The idea of small is a subjective notion and depends upon who you talk to and their needs. In *Fine Homebuilding*, Brian Pontolilo (2015) reiterates the idea that small is a relative term and as a publisher of an annual Best Small Home award limits participants to around 2000 square feet (185.80 square meters). He notes, Sarah Susanka, of *The Not So Big House* (2001) and other small house design books "talked us up to 2400 sq. ft [222.96 square meters] …"

This book offers guidance and suggestions in designing small interiors using affordable, ecologically responsible materials and methods. Clients are searching for ways and means to create a living environment that fosters a life of quality over quantity.

"Simplicity is about subtracting the obvious, and adding the meaningful," as Maeda (2015, ix) notes in *The Laws of Simplicity*.

Figure 1.2. The swimming pool adds to an indoor-outdoor ambiance that is important to the clients.

Source: Hole Photography, B. and H. Hartsock, Gar Rector and Associates.

RECOGNIZING ATTITUDES, VALUES, NEEDS AND EXPERIENCES

Whether designing small or large residences we advocate focus on the client's viewpoint, what they value and their desire to improve their living environment. We offer guidance in helping clients develop designs that share their uniqueness. In terms of living in smaller dwellings and living more simply, we offer ideas and solutions to create small homes that are individual, functional and aesthetic.

Some values and needs are not always obvious to clients. Our goal is to help you assist your clients in identifying these essential needs. We will share ideas about human factors, visual perception, visual impression and other experiences that influence preferences. We offer you a greater awareness of how many things your clients have and use in the course of a day that hold value over others. Then we'll give you exercises in the following chapters that will reveal what your clients might like to include in their small home design.

Human Factors

The relationship between the client and their home environment involves psychological and social needs such as privacy, personalized space, control of space and territoriality, particularly in small dwellings. Humans lay claim to areas and require different space proximities. Generally, intimate space distances range from 0 to 18 inches (.46 meters) and social distances, 4 feet (1.22 meters) to 12 feet (3.66 meters) (Pile 2003, 193). Socialization with friends and family are important functions and require attention to group interaction.

Consideration of ergonomics, as a human factor, requires adjustability of furnishings and other systems because of different sizes and abilities of family members. The International Ergonomics Association describes the domains of ergonomics: "Derived from the Greek ergon (work) and nomos (laws) to denote the science of work, ergonomics is a system-orientated discipline which now extends across all of human activity."

Physical human comfort requirements entail comfortable air temperature, humidity, air movement, acoustics and radiation control. Ventilation is a vital consideration, providing oxygen while removing carbon dioxide, odors and contaminants.

Order, variety and aesthetics are also important considerations. When clients are able to recognize and share important human factor information, the designer can manipulate the space with form, color, light and other elements to satisfy these human needs. To this end, we will explore needs and preferences in Chapter 2, *How to*

Help Clients Examine Their Own Situation, and address ways to design for these inclinations in Part 2 and Part 3.

Visual Perception

Design is an expressive tool that is used to communicate concepts and feelings. When we enter a space we move through each area, pausing here and there, taking in visual impressions with each step. We look up and down, side to side and sometimes in and out of other areas. This is how we perceive a space.

All of our sensory experiences define human interaction with our environments. An interior designer's job is to provide functionality in a small space as well as understand the importance of the

Figure 1.3. An eclectic chandelier mixed with traditional furnishings reflects the client's personality.

Source: Hole Photography, B. and H. Hartsock, Gar Rector and Associates/.

experience of the space. By considering the elements and principles of design such as color, light and textures, we can add to the client's involvement in the dwelling. Choice of materials, finishes, lighting, furniture, fixtures and equipment (FF&E), whether they be textiles or furnishing, contribute to the experience.

Figure 1.4. Colors create mood in this living room. Shapes and lines convey rhythm.

Source: Michael Hospelt Photography, WEISBACH architecture | design, Gar Rector and Associate.

Whatever materials or color scheme you choose, the design should be guided by the experience that you want for your client and the design concept that you have established. Use a well-developed design concept as your reference point. Design concepts are key ideas, formulated from understanding the client's needs and desires, the building and site, constraints and other abstract influences that prompt emotional responses. For example, the client's interest in artwork or nature might drive an overall theme or idea.

Visual Impression

We also form impressions in an environment that are emotional. We associate colors with mood, temperature and movement. Shapes and lines can convey feelings of rhythm or stability. The next time you are in an interior that is not your own, ask yourself how you feel in that room. What are the factors in the interior that influence your emotional response?

Chapters 4, 5 and 6 discuss the dynamics of design theory and the impressions resulting from elements and principles of design in an interior. Because of space constraints, small interiors require thoughtful planning on how a space will feel.

Experiences and Global Contexts

It is important for interior designers to be aware that clients have different experiences, which influence their attitudes, values and needs. Designers need to consider their clients' social, cultural, economic, geographical and ecological backgrounds – or a global view, when analyzing their clients' needs.

According to the CIDA's *Professional Standards 2017* (2016), it is worth the designer's while to be aware and understand how global context informs interior design. Designers should learn about a variety of cultural norms and events, and understand how they shape experiences and can influence interior design. Designers should listen carefully to their clients to understand how they react differently to space, colors, aesthetics and functionality. Case Study 4 illustrates how Team 7 International dealt with a variety of cultural differences in their design.

CHARACTERISTICS AND NEEDS OF DIFFERENT GENERATIONS: TRADITIONALS, BABY BOOMERS, GENERATION X, MILLENNIALS AND GENERATION Z

Figure 1.5. Different generations have different characteristics and needs.

Source: S. Halbe, P. and D. Bard.

Studies show that different generations have different characteristics and needs based on their particular experiences. By looking at Traditional, Baby Boomer, Generation X, Millennial and Generation Z generational needs, designers can gain a closer glimpse into those experiences.

In the business world, innovative firms look at generational characteristics and needs so that they can provide an environment that is productive and comfortable for all workers. Lancaster and

Stillman (2002) have given us insight into generational differences in *When Generations Collide: Who They Are. Why They Clash. How to Solve the Generational Puzzle at Work.*

More recently, Amy Smithers (2017), in *Will Generation Z Alter the Design of the Workplace?*, reports a year-long research study and the future of the workspace. Born between 1995 and 2010, the Gen Z generation describes themselves as social and tech-savvy.

Although the following characteristics and needs are very general, see how you and your client might fit in. You may be more like another generation than your own or a mix of generations. Remember, in the final analysis, all characteristics and needs are based on experiences and culture. In general, however, if we translate these preferences into the home, we might find that:

Traditionals, born in 1928–1945, develop their identity and put importance in their home. Many times their homes suggest their achievements. The American Society of Interior Designers' *Aging in Place Study*, which was conducted between 2000 and 2001, found that older Americans prefer to remain in their homes. Making the home functional and maintainable are important needs for this generation. We will discuss the dynamics of aging in place at the end of this chapter and include Case Study 1, *Phoenix Commons Condominiums.*

Baby Boomers, born between 1946 and 1964, are characterized by being team-oriented and optimistic. Individualistic, they are self-gratifying and like personal growth. They are interested in health and wellness, value youth and are exploring an engaged retirement. Baby Boomers do well in a blended environment of both private and open spaces that nurture their interests.

Generation X, born between 1965 and 1980, tend to be more informal, fun-loving and self-reliant. They are creative and entrepreneurial. They may be suited to flexible, multipurpose rooms with technological advancements. They like personal expression and the looks and quality of spaces.

Millennials, born after 1981 to the 2000s, are a nurtured generation characterized by being optimistic, civic-minded and confident. They have assets and challenges of multitasking. Virtual, social and interested in achieving, Millennials seem to like fun with open spaces that are flexible, functional and technological. A 2010 Pew Research Center study characterized this generation in the title, *Millennials: A Portrait of Generation Next: Confident. Connected. Open to Change.*

In Smither's (2017) report, Gen Zers need space for collaboration but want quiet space for work and telephone privacy. The most important characteristics in the workplace reported are comfort, calmness, cleanliness, mobility and flexibility.

NEED FOR UNIVERSAL, ACCESSIBLE, AGING IN PLACE, AND HEALTHY ENVIRONMENTS

Universal design says it all. We all have a need for it. According to Mitton and Nystuen (2016, 7), in *Residential Interior Design*, universal design is, "The design of all products and environments to be as usable as possible by as many people as possible regardless of age, ability, or situation." We need to identify clients' requirements no matter what generation they represent or what they need.

A growing number of Baby Boomers have been expanding market needs for smaller dwellings. Many of them have downsized from large family homes to smaller homes in order to lessen upkeep and accommodate physical challenges.

Baby Boomers are an active senior population, seeking homes that provide them with greater independence and a higher quality of life.

Safe and affordable neighborhoods, accessibility to medical services and engaging entertainment are high on their requirement lists. They want their "last" homes to have aging-in-place features to support increasing physical challenges as they grow older. Aging-in-place design looks at ways the client can remain in their current home rather than moving to a senior facility or a place of institutional care.

It is important to understand universal, accessible, aging-in-place, and healthy environmental design in relation to small dwellings. Case Study 1 describes condominiums that exemplify homes with these designed qualities. Case Study 4, in Chapter 3, illustrates design solutions for a homeowner's environmental sensitivities and health. With an increased awareness of well-being and health requirements, designers can incorporate healthy goals by following the WELL Building Standard and International WELL Building Institute performance requirements for buildings. Seven categories of design standards relate to human health and consider air, water, nourishment, light, fitness, comfort and mind attributes (Viani 2016, 37).

Designers can make a space work functionally as well as aesthetically and emotionally. We will help you identify your clients' needs in the following chapters and offer design solutions in Part 2.

"Recognizing the need is the primary condition for design." (Hartman and Demetrios, 2007, *100 Quotes from Charles Eames.*)

CASE STUDY 1: PHOENIX COMMONS, DEVELOPER CHRISTIAN ZIMMERMAN, ARCHITECT JEFF ZIMMERMAN, ZIMMERMAN AND ASSOCIATES, OAKLAND, CALIFORNIA, USA, 2016

Phoenix Commons, a Leadership in Energy and Environmental Design (LEED)-certified building, is located in the Jingletown Arts

Figure 1.6. Phoenix Commons, a LEED certified building.

Source: C. Zimmerman, Architect, Zimmerman and Associates, Treve Johnson Photography.

District area in Oakland, California. It was developed as a site for a senior cohousing community. Aging-in-place features as well as communal spaces for social engagement were the primary needs for this project. Residents own their individual, small condominiums.

Artist lofts, cafes, condominiums and warehouses share space in this mixed-use neighborhood. Medical services, social venues as well as public transportation are located within walking distance to Alameda Island, just a walk across the bridge outside of the building.

The design concept of this building was to provide residents opportunities to create a community using the cohousing model of living. Cohousing, which was developed in Denmark, promotes autonomous living within private dwellings with the support of a close, accessible community of neighbors. Social support and shared resources and activities, such as community meals, keep seniors engaged with each other and reduce isolation.

Figure 1.7. Medical services, social venues as well as public transportation are located within walking distance to Alameda Island.

Source: C. Zimmerman, Architect, Zimmerman and Associates, K. Turcznski.

Communal rooms for socializing, dining, cooking, exercise and meetings are located on the first floor. Each residential floor has a separate room for individual or group use.

Inclusive design solutions are found throughout the building. Latch handles for doors, kitchen and bathrooms are present in all rooms. Non-slip flooring such as Marmoleum, low-pile carpeting or vinyl flooring was used for interiors. Textured concrete and rubberized strips are on walkways and stair steps. Wide entrances to all rooms accommodate wheelchair access. Large shower stalls with low thresholds diminish possibilities for tripping and provides room for seating as the need arises.

Figure 1.8. Communal rooms provide opportunities for social interactions.

Source: C. Zimmerman, Architect, Zimmerman and Associates, Treve Johnson Photography.

Figure 1.9. Universal design such as latch handles are found throughout the building.

Source: R. Mark.

Figure 1.10. An atrium floor plan with windows facing walkways provides residents with passive and interactive social contact.

Source: C. Zimmerman, Architect, Zimmerman and Associates, K. Turcznski.

An atrium floor plan with windows facing walkways provides residents passive or interactive social engagement. Kitchen windows face the atrium for more public viewing while the living room is located further back to provide more privacy. Large tall windows are abundant throughout the building, providing natural light and views to nature.

Each unit has individual thermostat controls to save energy. Lights and fans can be controlled remotely to aid visual and dexterity issues. Windows in all rooms provide good airflow.

A walking path alongside the Oakland estuary borders one side of the building. Residents are able to commune with nature through bird watching, dog walking or moments of peaceful reflection sitting alongside the waterway.

INTERVIEW WITH JEFF ZIMMERMAN, ARCHITECT

What Instigated the Idea of Phoenix Commons?

My partner, Christian, and I reflected on the need for less institutional living environments for seniors. Christian has developed and owns several nursing and assisted-living communities. He wanted to provide ownership housing for middle-income seniors. I wanted seniors to spend more time outside of their home and actively engage with the world. We both wanted opportunities for more community engagement for seniors.

Figure 1.11. Walking paths along estuary provide viewing of waterways and visiting birds.

Source: C. Zimmerman, Architect, Zimmerman and Associates, K. Turcznski.

What Conditions Drove Your Design Concept and Programming?

The Phoenix Commons design concept was based on the site of the property. It was situated at the end of a block that had been derelict for a number of years. One side had a unique green draw-bridge where cars busily funneled into two lanes on the way to the freeway. A cement plant was in view a block away with a backdrop of boats along an estuary. Another side faced a run-down building with peeling paint. The third side faced a peaceful estuary with a walking path alongside the water.

The site had an urban edge of roughness and natural beauty. I wanted to create a mild chaotic environment where the different elements would blur and pulse providing a variety of senses for the residents.

What Other Ideas Did the Location Prompt?

I wanted to bring the outdoors indoors. Tall windows in all communal and private areas allow views of outdoor space. The main lounge and dining room face the estuary where passing tugboats, rowers and assorted boats pass by. Shorebirds and occasional seal

Figure 1.12. Areas of both high energy and peaceful movement are seen outside of the building.

Source: C. Zimmerman, Architect, Zimmerman and Associates, K. Turcznski.

sightings bring nature to their doorstep. Some units have windows that provide views of the workings going on in the cement factory while others can see ships enter the estuary. There are areas of both high energy and slow peaceful movement outside the building. Residents can partake by looking through windows or stepping outside their door.

Figure 1.13. Communal rooms accommodate large and intimate gatherings.

Source: C. Zimmerman, Architect, Zimmerman and Associates, K. Turcznski.

Phoenix Commons Feels Like a Neighborhood. How Did You Design For This?

I envisioned homes that had front porches where people would want to communicate with each other. Each condominium unit faces an open atrium where residents can see neighbors walk by. They can passively or actively engage with each other. All units have flow-through space in front and back with windows on each side. In every unit, the kitchen faces the atrium for public engagement. The living room is located in the rear of the unit to provide privacy.

On the main floor, communal rooms vary in size to accommodate large meetings or intimate gatherings. Each residential floor has a common room for small gatherings, meditation or quiet workspace.

What Other Concepts were Important to the Design?

Inclusive design. Aging-in-place features are everywhere in the building. Large bathrooms, wide entrances for wheelchair access, low thresholds in showers, latch handles for arthritic hands, textured outdoor flooring, low-impact interior flooring and remote control lighting are some of the inclusive design features in place as the needs arise for residents.

How Long Did the Design Process Take?

The project was completed within 18 months.

REFERENCES

American Society of Interior Designers. *Aging in Place: Aging and the Impact of Interior Design.* [Based on The Aging in Place Study conducted between 2000 and 2001.]

Council for Interior Design Accreditation Professional Standards. 2016. "Professional Standards 2017." https://accredit-id.org/wp-content/uploads/2017/01/II.-Professional-Standards-2017.pdf.

Hartman, Carla and Eames Demetrios, eds. 2007. *100 Quotes from Charles Eames.* Santa Monica, CA: A Publication of Eames Office.

International Ergonomics Association. "Definition and Domains of Ergonomics." Accessed April 4, 2017. www.iea.cc/whats/index.html.

Lancaster, Lynne C. Stillman, and David Stillman. 2002. *When Generations Collide: Who They Are. Why They Clash. How to Solve the Generational Puzzle at Work.* New York, NY: HarperCollins.

Maeda, John. 2015. *The Laws of Simplicity.* Cambridge, MA: MIT Press. ix.

Mitton, Maureen and Courtney Nystuen 2016. *Residential Interior Design: A Guide to Planning Spaces*, 3rd ed. Hoboken, NJ: John Wiley & Sons, Inc. 7.

Pew Research Center. 2010. *Millennials: A Portrait of Generation Next: Confident. Connected. Open to Change.* www.pewsocialtrends.org/files/2010/10/millennials-condident-connected-open-to.pdf.

Pile, John F. 2003. *Interior Design*, 3rd ed. Upper Saddle River, NJ: Prentice-Hall, Inc. 193.

Pontolilo, Brian. 2015. *Fine Homebuilding.* "What's the Difference? Small Home vs. Tiny House." Accessed July 13, 2017. www.finehomebuilding.com/2015/01/14/whats-the-difference-small-home-vs-tiny-house.

Smithers, Amy. 2017. *Will Generation Z Alter the Design of the Workplace?* DesignCurial. Accessed August 8, 2017. www.designcurial.com/news/the-future-of-the-workplace-5823716.

Susanka, Sarah with Kira Obolensky. 2001. *The Not So Big House: A Blueprint for the Way We Really Live.* Newtown, CT: Taunton Press, Inc.

Viani, Lisa Owens. 2016. *ASID ICON.* "A Healthier Hive." Washington, DC (Fall). 37.

## CHAPTER 2

HOW TO HELP CLIENTS EXAMINE THEIR OWN SITUATION

THE IMPORTANCE OF IDENTIFYING CLIENTS' UNIQUE NEEDS AND WANTS

Your clients' viewpoints matter. What they value and desire for their home is what this book is about. "All of the basic human needs are satisfied there [the home], including individual ones (for example, self-esteem and autonomy) and social ones (for example, love and affection)" (Miller and Schlitt 1985, 2).

How does a person recognize what they need and what would make their home feel just right? A good designer looks beyond trends and styles and investigates who will inhabit the dwelling. The designer interviews, observes and in general deeply delves into the client's everyday life.

Figure 2.1. A good designer looks beyond trends and styles and investigates who will inhabit the dwelling.

Source: C. Barry.

The client with the designer can explore what composes the client's life in terms of choice of lifestyle and things that are important to him. Human factors, generational needs and other values, as discussed in Chapter 1, are investigated. The client and designer can jointly create a living environment that is meaningful to the client.

PARTICIPATORY DESIGN

Participatory design is an approach that is inclusive. It involves the client partnering with the designer to create an interior or building that meets the emotional and functional needs of the client. It is codesigning.

Inclusive design tries to understand the needs of all potential users of a space and to provide for these needs. It ensures that people are put at the center of the design process and responds to human diversity in a positive way. It provides the individual, whatever their abilities, with freedom, dignity, and choice about the way they live their lives, and it delivers spaces that retain flexibility of use.
(Dodsworth and Anderson 2015, 114)

The relationship between designer and client involves active listening and a dialogue between the two parties. Programming techniques, as presented in this book, open pathways for discussion that help clients gain clarity and focus on what is important and what holds less value.

Participatory design is beneficial in providing the client with greater understanding of what is meaningful to them and a feeling of ownership in the planning of their home. Secondly, you will gain the benefit of establishing a closer relationship with your client; learning about individual nuances of how culture, background and history have shaped their choices.

Creating an interior that supports the inner needs of an individual can provide a structure that is grounded. The heart and hearth of the home should provide elements that hold the individual secure within.

With that, we provide a client questionnaire to get started when you interview your client. You can use the worksheets found in Appendix A. You might want to read *Case Study 2: A Condominium for Rose*, a programming interview between Rose and Sherrill, to get an idea of where we are going with this exercise. This process can be informative and useful in your planning.

EXPLORING THE CLIENT'S LIVING SITUATION

Example of a Questionnaire for the Client – Examining Their Situation

1. List characteristics about who you are and your related needs. For example, interview yourself and write down your age, socioeconomic status, community needs and physical conditions including if you are right- or left-handed and if you have vision or hearing needs. If you have other family members, write down the same characteristics for them. Do you live in a multigenerational household?

Example: Age 53, female; semi-retired; active in gardening, yoga and running; volunteer work; nearsighted; left-handed;

... Age 56, male ...

2. Ask yourself where you would like to live. Mark down possibilities such as living in a house, a condo or an apartment. Would you consider an existing structure or would you design a new structure? Would you live in a house with a yard, a communal building with communal land or in living quarters above a commercial building? Would roof gardens or decks or garden walls be possible? Consider the possibilities.

Figure 2.2. A rock wall softened by plants and a fireplace provides a sense of privacy, comfort and warmth.

Source: Calistoga Ranch Auberge Spa, S. Halbe.

Example: I would prefer to live in a detached house in the country with great views. Plants and a garden are important to me ...

3. List values that matter to you. For example, do you value nature and green principles? Do you have spiritual beliefs? Do you value humor and fun-loving activities? Are friendships important to you, including pets? Do you value quality over quantity?

Figure 2.3. Provide a quiet place for resting.

Source: Sherrill Baldwin Halbe Interior Design, S. Halbe.

Example: I love to entertain. I host intimate dinner parties and an occasional cocktail party for a larger group ...

4. How do you feel about privacy, personalized space, control of space and territoriality? Do you value order, variety, aesthetics, or socialization with friends and family cohesiveness? Make a list of the conditions that are important to you and write down where in your house you would especially like to experience these conditions.

Example: I'd like to have a quiet place just to sit, read or think

5. Consider when you can put a plan in place. Some people build, remodel, or accessorize in phases. Prioritize your needs, your budget and convenient timing. List your immediate needs and figure out what you can afford. Then list your future needs and desires. If you have a written plan you are more likely to go forward and realize your goals. When you list your needs and desires make note of future changes that might occur.

Example: I will need room for my mother as she gets older and spends more time with us. My son will go to college, but will spend summers here.

"I have come to believe that 1. Our sense of self and sense of the environment are intimately and profoundly entwined; ..."
(Israel 2010, ix–x)

CASE STUDY 2: AN INTERVIEW – A CONDOMINIUM FOR ROSE, OAKLAND, CALIFORNIA, USA, 2014

We thought that you might find the following interview helpful. Let's listen in. Rose is going through the process of designing her

624 square feet (57.98 square meters) condominium at Phoenix Commons. Sherrill is interviewing Rose to help identify her needs and desires, which will help in writing a program for Rose's small dwelling design. You can find Rose's Program in Appendix C.

After you have considered what is important to your client, go ahead and read Chapter 3 and start writing a "program." Remember, this is an ongoing process so when you think of other important aspects you can add them to your list.

A Dialogue Between Sherrill and Rose

R: I want my living environment to reflect who I am as well as meet my physical needs for now and as I age. I'm on a fixed income with a small budget for home improvement and I want to use as much of what I already have rather than purchase all new furniture.

R: I've read a number of books and magazines on decorating but I don't know how to use this information. There's so much out there, it's all a mish-mosh of stuff that I can't afford or is too complicated to figure out. It's overwhelming and I don't know how to apply it to my own space. I don't know where to place my sofa and chairs so they look interesting and are functional. They just look boring wherever I place them. How do I figure this out? I don't know where and how to start. I don't have a sense of design but I know what I like.

S: Let's start with good design. Design is a plan and the first step in planning is to identify what you want. We look at existing conditions, what you have and what you want to include in your life and translate this information into a design for your physical dwelling.

S: Design using a holistic method is usually more successful than piecemeal planning. A holistic approach looks at all of the needed parts of the plan to make the design come together and form a whole. We need to consider not only functional and aesthetic needs but emotional considerations.

R: Does holistic planning mean I have to buy or have all the furniture for the whole house?

S: No, we need to look at all of the parts of the whole plan. First, let's look at the floor plan of your condominium unit to see how individual pieces of furniture can fit into the rooms. We'll need measurements for each room. With this information we'll be able to see which pieces of furniture can fit into the rooms.

S: Next, we need to identify existing physical conditions that are stationary. These would be the windows, doors, closets, cabinetry, lighting, outlets and built-ins. We will include large appliances such as dishwasher, refrigerator and stove.

For example, we can identify things like one ceiling light fixture in the living room, two outlets in the dining room, one large window and four small windows on the south side of the dining room.

R: How am I going to fit furniture that filled a house that was more than twice the size of what I'm moving into?

S: We'll look at how much space is in each room. You'll be listing all the furniture you have, their function and your needs for each room. With this information and the measurements of each room you'll be able to choose which pieces you need.

R: I can't afford to buy all the pieces I need at the same time. How can I do this?

S: Once you have a clear picture of what is needed and what will fit in each room, you'll be able to focus and easily find each new piece. Take your time choosing and acquiring each piece. Like a book, you are creating a story for each room. Think of it as a treasure hunt for that special piece. You might find it at a flea market, estate sale, consignment store or even a neighborhood furniture store. A family or friend might be culling their furnishings and thank you for taking it off their hands.

R: How do I make my interiors reflect me? I've torn out pictures in magazines with the colors and kind of furniture I like but I'm either too afraid to use those colors or can't afford the furniture.

S: You have a number of items that reflect who you are already. After completing the planning program you'll have a better idea of how to fit them in your rooms and what you need. Let's do an exercise to help you get in touch with your emotional needs for your home.

S: Thinking of your home, what do you dream about in terms of colors, shapes and textures?

R: I dream about a Moroccan red wall, a sectional, a kitchen and dining room that feels exciting and energizing, a peaceful serene bedroom with really luxurious bedding, a kitchen painted turmeric yellow. It's a dream of course, since the space will be so small and the colors are too bold.

S: You can actually have strong colors in small spaces. It's just how and where you use the colors.

R: What about a turmeric yellow kitchen? A dark, azure blue bathroom?

S: Absolutely. We'll look at the amount of space you'll have available in those rooms and plan how much and where you can use these colors.

R: Wow! Really?

S: What are some things that you need to have in your rooms?

R: I need to have specific spaces to place objects, my own personal comfortable chair, quiet places, lots of light, no glare, a feeling of openness, a place to be alone, color.

S: Imagine you are entering your house. What would you like to see?

R: I want colors, shapes and objects that express our curiosity and love of life.

I want the walls in the entrance, living room and dining area to be Moroccan red.

I want the backsplash in the kitchen to be turmeric yellow and I want other colors in the kitchen to express our enjoyment of cooking all the different cuisines that we love so much.

S: Great! Now that we have ideas of what you need emotionally and aesthetically we can look at the functional needs list and create a design plan that meets these areas. So work on getting the items of your list down and we'll create a design plan for your home.

REFERENCES

Dodsworth, Simon and Stephen Anderson. 2015. *The Fundamentals of Interior Design*, 2nd Ed. London: Fairchild Books. 114.

Israel, Toby. 2010. *Some Place Like Home: Using Design Psychology to Create Ideal Places*. Princeton, NJ: Design Psychology Press. ix–x.

Miller, Stuart and Judith K. Schlitt. 1985. *Interior Space: Design Concepts for Personal Needs*. New York, NY: Praeger. 2.

## CHAPTER 3

SMALL DWELLING PROGRAMMING FOR CLIENTS

Figure 3.1. This kitchen required keen programming analysis and identification.

Source: Michael Hospelt Photography, WEISBACH architecture | design, Gar Rector and Associates.

PROGRAMMING

One of the most important steps in designing is to create a Program. Programming for small spaces is a vital process of analyzing and identifying what is needed in the design, what already exists, the budget and what may be needed in the future. Programming is essential in identifying unique needs, dreams and future goals.

How does one go about doing this? Sometimes the obvious doesn't occur to clients. Sometimes it feels overwhelming. Many times clients won't voice their preferences because it goes against modern trends or preconceived ideas of what works and doesn't work in a home.

We have provided programming exercises with examples for you and your client's use and worksheets in the resource section at the back of the book. In Appendix A you will find forms to be filled out by the client and separate forms for the interior designer's use.

We will start with recording a daily routine followed by taking an inventory of the client's furnishings and accessories. These two exercises show which belongings are essential and which are no longer needed. The essential, desired and future needs exercise demonstrates what your client must keep, what they hope to include, and a plan for changing needs. The physical interior elements exercise will help your client recognize fixed and built-in objects such as lighting, plumbing and electrical needs. The *Building in Context* exercise addresses climatic orientation, proximity to noise and accessibility to nature. The *Function of Each Room* exercise gives a greater awareness of how each room provides different physical and emotional needs. Spatial planning, color, lighting, texture and other design features can influence the function and emotional responses of each room. We will also discuss universal design issues as well as aging in place, healthy environment issues and budget questions.

Because budget costs vary from one place to another the designer must stay alert to the areas' refurbishing, remodeling and building figures. Costs also change from time to time. Go online and check out local indexes and trade reports.

The designer can help their client estimate costs based on general factors. Depending on the scope of the project, Pile (2007) outlines basic costs as consisting of construction contracts, purchases and installation, fees and other costs such as permits and contingencies. The designer must rely on research and experience to guide the client when determining and scheduling their budget.

It is important that the designer obtains the client's budgeting information early in the programming phase (Ballast 2010). The client may have a set budget and may not know the costs involved with their particular project. The designer can ascertain the client's needs, resources and desires by having a conversation with the client early on. It is helpful to know how the client wants to spend their money. Budget exercises and examples will get you started.

DAILY ROUTINE WORKSHEET FOR THE CLIENT

The Daily Routine Worksheet helps you become more conscious of what tools and furnishings you use in your daily life. Our example illustrates how you can use the worksheets.

Example:

AM: turn off alarm clock, walk dog, toilet, shower, use lotions on body, put on makeup, put on tea kettle, make tea/coffee, eat breakfast, clean up, run errands or work at laptop

Midday: Listen to music on CDs, prepare lunch, run errands as needed, read research literature and write on laptop. Do laundry as needed

PM: Walk dog, prepare meal, eat, clean up, read, watch news on TV, watch International Mystery at 9:00 PM

INVENTORY OF FURNISHINGS AND ACCESSORIES FOR THE CLIENT AND DESIGNER

What do you have in each room? List the number, description, color and material of each furnishing and accessory that you have in each room. **The designer can add dimensions and other characteristics to this form later. Please note if a lighting fixture is moveable or stationary.

Example:

Furnishings and Accessories in the Living Room

#	Description	Color	Material	**W, H, D	Other
1	Chaise Sofa	Green	Velveteen		
1	Sofa Bed	White	Cloth		
1	Bertoia Chair	White	Cloth		
1	Table Lamp	Gold	Brass		

Furnishings and Accessories in the Dining Room

Example

#	Description	Color	Material	**W, H, D	Other
1	Oak Table	Light			

ESSENTIAL, DESIRED AND FUTURE NEEDS FOR THE CLIENT

Think of all of your household needs even if they seem impossible to include in a small space. Every square inch counts, so there are ways to accommodate what is important to you. Arrange your list of priorities as to what is essential and what is desired. Prioritize what is needed now and what you will need in the future. Will you have special requirements when you are older or will a child or older person be living with you at a later time?

Example:

Bedroom

Essential needs	Desired needs	Future needs
Bed	Dressing Table	
Bed Table	Media Center	
Chair(s)	Armoire	Ottoman

Lamps

PHYSICAL INTERIOR ELEMENTS FOR THE CLIENT

Look at your existing dwelling and its physical interior elements such as lighting, outlets, windows, doors, and structural and non-structural partitions. Write down physical interior elements that you might like to change.

Example:

Bedroom

Possible Changes

Two outlets on each wall
Sliding doors instead of closet with
   swinging doors

In Appendix A you will find separate forms for the interior designer to record existing physical interior elements.

BUILDING IN CONTEXT FOR THE CLIENT*

For your existing dwelling, take note of all of its physical exterior elements. Include things like sun orientation (what side of the house gets the morning sun?), natural settings and accessibility to the outdoors, climate orientation (what's the weather like?), scenery, etc.

Take note of those characteristics. Write down what you like and what might be changed.

Examples:

First of all, what places in nature are you drawn to? Places like mountains, water, parks, forest, woods?

I love the mountains and water

How do you feel about sustainability? What are your needs?

I want all materials as sustainable as possible.
I need a place for recycling

Tell us about the outside of your home:

Sun orientation (what side of the house gets the morning sun?)

East side

Natural settings and accessibility to the outdoors

Flower pots and fields seen from my windows. I have decks

Climate orientation – what's the weather like?

Four seasons: Hot in the summer and can be very cold in the winter. Wind from the west

Scenery

Great scenes from my windows of mountains and sunsets

Urban, suburban, rural setting

Rural but close to town

Noise levels

Quiet

Style or characteristic of the exterior of your home

Cedar siding; Shed roof

*In Appendix A you will find separate forms for the interior designer to record additional contextual information.

WHAT FUNCTION DOES EACH ROOM PROVIDE FOR THE CLIENT?

Each room serves physical and emotional functions. Here are checklists for each room. What do you want to do in that room? What kind of mood do you want this room to satisfy?

Example:

Bedroom

Physical   *Sleep, rest, watch TV, read*

Emotional   *A place to sleep and relax. A quiet, soothing place; a place to get away from activity*

Living Room

Physical   *Watch TV, read, listen to music, entertain*

Emotional   *A place to relax where stimulating conversations and exchange of ideas would take place*

Dining Room

Physical   *A place to eat meals, study, prep meals, spread out work papers, entertain, need good, adjustable lighting*

Emotional   *A chameleon room that can change with the emotions of those using it. For example, it might be peaceful and quiet for intimate meals or colorful, noisy and exciting with company*

Kitchen

Physical   *Organized spaces to prep, cook, eat, clean, keep tools and appliances*

Emotional   *Lively, colorful, full of life and excitement*

Bathroom

Physical   *Easy to clean, no clutter, good lighting*

Emotional   *Peaceful, like a spa*

Other Rooms (such as an office or a second bedroom)

Physical   *A second bedroom might double as a guest room and an art room*

Emotional   *Inspirational room with pin boards of favorite pictures*

AESTHETIC DESIRES FOR THE CLIENT

Think about your fantasies and what would give you emotional satisfaction. The aesthetics of color, texture and shapes can express themselves in fabric, furnishings and architectural detail.

Example:

Bedroom

I've always wanted:

I have always wanted a dusty rose table skirt and a rustic barn door in a room. Why? I'm not sure but these things make me feel happy. Perhaps they carry associations from my past; a kind of patina of days gone by. The soft, refined feel of silk contrasted with various sheens and shades of hard wood stimulate my senses and bring back memories of my girlhood growing up in Montana.

I dream about these objects, furniture and architectural details in my environment:

Silk table skirt
A barn door-style divider

What colors spring to mind in this room?

Dusty rose
Brown to black
Creamy warm off-white
Lots of colorful oil paintings

UNIVERSAL, ACCESSIBLE, AGING IN PLACE, AND HEALTHY ENVIRONMENTAL DESIGN FOR THE CLIENT

Do you have any specific needs to be included in your design for now or the future? Do you have allergies or sensitivities to types of flooring, materials or lighting? Do you have or will you need additional space requirements for medical equipment? Do you need special hardware for present or future health needs?

Specific Health Needs for Present and Future

Example:

I am allergic or sensitive to these types of building materials.

I am sensitive to fluorescent light. The fumes from most paints and certain flooring materials affect my respiratory system.

I need or will need aging-in-place hardware on doors, cabinets and other fixtures.

I would like shower grab bars installed to give me extra support. I need door latches and levers that are large and easy to use since I have arthritis in my hands.

I need or will need additional space for medical equipment.

I don't need anything right now but would like entrances to rooms wide enough to accommodate wheelchairs for friends or me.

BUDGET AND SCHEDULING FOR THE CLIENT

Think about a realistic budget. What monies do you have available now and what might you have in the future? You don't need to purchase everything at the same time. Take time to explore the type of furniture or accessory that will fit in with your dream design. The clearer you are in knowing what you want, the easier it will be to find it. Prioritize what items you want to purchase new and what you are open to buying second-hand. This will save you money.

Budgeting and Scheduling Exercise Example

What is the scope of your project?

I want to choose furnishings and flooring for my new condo.

What is your spending range for your project as you see it now?

I would like to spend between $5000 and $10,000. I would like to install a fireplace if there is money left over.

Do you have accessible money for your project?

I have a home equity loan.

Will you have future funds for your project?

I may have inheritance money.

Are you willing to do your project in phases or do you want to do it all at once?

Phases are okay.

Based on the information that we have obtained from the other exercises, what would you want to do now? What is your time frame?

I am willing to have a fireplace later. I need basic living room furniture now. I'd like to furnish the living room before Christmas.

Based on the information that we have obtained from other exercises, when would you want to implement future plans?

In five years.

When you choose your furnishings, fixtures, equipment, materials and finishes will you spend more for function, sustainability or how it looks?

I will spend more for sustainable features. I want a really stylish recliner and will spend more. I don't care if the tile is cheaper.

When you choose your furnishings, fixtures, equipment, materials and finishes do you want to stay in a high, mid or low price range?

Mostly midrange except for sustainable features and the recliner

When you choose your furnishings, fixtures, equipment, materials and finishes do you want to consider quality over a set price range?

For some things I like quality and will pay the price.

If you are trying to stay in a certain range are you okay with a mix of high, mid and low end items?

Yes.

If you have an amount in mind are you willing to look at options out of your price range?

I'm willing to look at them.

Are you willing to look at options below your price range?

Yes.

For example:

Check out local furniture stores to find one what will fit your style, price range and quality standards. Visit them from time to time for sales.

Junk yards, charity shops, consignment shops, flea markets, eBay, Craigslist are great places to find well-made used furniture and accessories. Friends can also be great resources as they may want to get rid of a piece or know someone who has that particular piece that you are looking for.

Rose

I've always wanted a sectional. I knew I wanted one that had open legs in order to provide a more open spacious look in my living room. After looking through consignment and charity stores I realized that what I wanted needed to be new. Another item was a gate-leg dining room table. I'd seen a number of them in consignment stores and junk yards so I felt confident I could find the one I wanted in one of those places. I also wanted a bench I could use for seating as well as for a landing area. I had seen one at a friend's home and was referred to a local furniture store.

This is what I ended up with: A used gate-leg table that had three leaves from a local junk *yard. Unopened it would fit four; with the addition of three leaves it seated 12 people. I got it for a steal at $70. At a local consignment shop I found a small gate-leg table for our tiny kitchen. It would seat two and we could use it as a prepping table. It cost me $30. At the Salvation Army I found a beautiful Oriental lamp with a base that had all the tones of my color scheme. That beauty cost me $15. The only thing I needed to add was a new lampshade, which I took from a lamp I no longer liked. The bench that I wanted happened to be on sale for $109. A small glass top end table came from my friend, Therese, for free. I had given her a number of my furniture so this was a great exchange.*

With the money saved from the best buys, I had a bit more money available to purchase the rest of the things on my list. I decided to take my time purchasing the rest, hoping that perhaps they might go on sale.

With the information gathered from these exercises you can write your Program. We have provided a Program Template in Appendix B. You can also look at a sample program, *A Program for Rose* in Appendix C, which was based on the interview between Sherrill and Rose in Case Study 2.

The next case study demonstrates attributes of programming for small dwellings. Case Study 3 describes how a homeowner considered her environmental sensitivities and health when planning a new single-family detached home. In *Case Study 5, Little House on the Prairie*, we illustrate how programming was used to spotlight needs and design for multipurpose solutions.

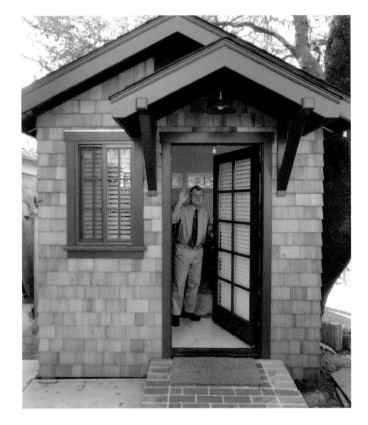

Figure 3.2. Man feels
at home.

Source: S. Halbe, Gar Rector
and Associates.

**There is one timeless way of building. It is a
thousand years old, and the same today as it has
ever been. The great traditional buildings of the past,
the villages and tents and temples in which man
feels at home, have always been made by people
who were very close to the center of this way.**
(Alexander 1979,7)

Design is like a puzzle. You lay out all of the parts and put them
together to reflect the client's own exceptional story. By doing this,
a certain originality and aesthetic emerges resulting in comfort and
their own special expression.

CASE STUDY 3: MOUNTAIN VIEW HOUSE, HOMEOWNERS WARREN AND DONNA HIEBERT, BUILDER WILDE CONSTRUCTION, VISSER ARCHITECTS, GALLATIN GATEWAY, MONTANA, USA, 2016

Mountain View House is located on a ridge overlooking a Montana ranch and the Gallatin mountain range. Donna, an active, petite Baby Boomer, had the small 900 square feet (83.61 square meters) dwelling built to her specification for wellness and health. The home is on her son's acreage, but draws privacy from the contours of the plains.

The design concept for the home embraces views of an active working ranch and southern mountains as well as reflecting the

Figure 3.3. Mountain View House.

Source: W. and D. Hiebert, L. Barber.

owner's value of a sustainable and healthy environment. Universal design was a major criterion in the plan that addressed the owner's sensitivities to indoor air quality and physical obstacles and her desire to age in place. An energetic resident, she needed a place to continue her lifestyle of entertaining, accommodating her grandchildren's sleepovers and healing in comfort.

Donna's budget was a consideration and she carefully shopped for local, reasonably priced fixtures and appliances that were both energy-efficient and environmentally healthy. She worked closely with her contractor, who appreciated and considered her limited resources and environmental sensitivities. Donna designed around most of her existing furnishings, choosing finishes, colors and textures accordingly.

Figure 3.4. Finishes, colors and textures were chosen to highlight existing furnishings.

Source: W. and D. Hiebert, L. Barber.

INTERVIEW: HOMEOWNER DONNA HIEBERT

The interior spaces are open and bright with incredible views yet are warm and fresh within the space. What were your considerations when choosing materials and finishes to accommodate your environmental sensitivities?

I was diagnosed with an environmental illness by the Mayo Clinic. It is important that I am not further subjected to volatile organic compounds and fluorescent lighting. Some of the consequences of my sensitivities are balance, temperature and mobility irregularities. My environment needs to be warm and I need to be able to negotiate steps, manipulate levers and drawers and avoid visual obstructions such as large patterns and flickering lights.

It was important that I build my small home in this area so that I could control my exposure to typical neighborhood pesticides and fumes. Standard condo materiality and building techniques were also a problem. Some of the design solutions that were employed were: radiant heat and a consistent texture in the concrete flooring; no VOC's in structural materials, furnishing, fixtures and equipment; incandescent lighting and circulation fans – without lighting; and operable drawers and hardware with levers and large handles. I chose a countertop material that was not cold to the touch and I took advantage of passive warmth from the southeastern window exposure. I made sure that appliances were easy to manipulate such as a pull-out dishwasher and in general an environment where my body can be calm and at rest. In addition the sauna and massage table provide heat and body relief and the walk-in shower alleviates a step.

Figure 3.5. Details were designed specifically for the client's height.

Source: W. and D. Hiebert, L. Barber.

How does an environmentally healthy home fit in with your plan of aging in place?

The great thing about all of the healthy environmental solutions that I mentioned is that I can live here a long time. If I need wheelchair accessibility or a walker, my home will be accommodating.

We built the shower with additional support under the tile for a future fold-down shower bench and Americans with Disabilities Act (ADA)-style grab bars. In addition, the contractor included details that were designed specifically for my height.

I love being in my home – I look out my windows at cattle grazing, deer wandering close to the house and the colors of the mountains at different times of day. I want to be here as long as I can.

Figure 3.6. Sustainable materiality such as stained concrete flooring provides healthier living spaces.

Source: W. and D. Hiebert, L. Barber.

I know that you wanted a sustainable home. How did you incorporate "green" ideas in a small house?

These are the big things for me: reclaim, reuse, resource locally and use the healthiest, most natural materials as possible. All these things will help the environment and will also create healthier living spaces. For example, I purchased my comfortable, natural mattress from a local manufacturer and the mattress is environmentally healthy.

We sourced local, custom details of cabinetry, the barn door and other interior doors and woodwork. Steel and retaining wall blocks were produced locally.

Figure 3.7. The client sourced local cabinetry, the barn door and other interior doors and woodwork.

Source: W. and D. Hiebert, L. Barber.

Because the house is small I needed to incorporate flexibility and multifunctionality. For example, the moveable barn door divides the living room from the bedroom entrance as well as hides the television set and built-in cupboards.

To Alexander, the goal of good architecture is to achieve a Kabalist–Taoist "quality without a name": buildings, towns, and gardens that make us feel most alive, the most true to ourselves, the most unselfconscious, the most whole, the most complete, the most free. The person capable of achieving this quality is ... an everyman or everywoman, full of innocence and devoid of ego ...
(Sheen 2017 in reviewing Christopher Alexander's 1979 seminal book, *The Timeless Way of Building*)

Figure 3.8. An attractive moveable barn door divides the living room from the bedroom entrance.

Source: W. and D. Hiebert, L. Barber.

Figure 3.9. Achieving a rewarding life in a small dwelling.

Source: Hole Photography, B. and H. Hartsock, Gar Rector and Associates.

One can achieve a rewarding intentional life, even in a small dwelling. With close needs analysis and conscientious planning, you can design a significant home for your clients. Equipped with knowing what they want, we will guide you in Part 2 when designing their space.

REFERENCES

Alexander, Christopher. 1979. *Timeless Way of Building*. New York, NY: Oxford University Press. 7.

Ballast, David Kent, FAIA. 2010. *Interior Design Reference Manual: Everything You Need to Know to Pass the NCIDQ Exam*.

Pile, John F. 2007. *Interior Design*. Upper Saddle River, NJ: Pearson Education, Inc.

Sheen, David. "The Timeless Way of Building." *Anarchiteture: firstearth@ davidsheen.com*. Accessed April 4, 2017. www.davidsheen.com/words/ timeless.htm.

Part 2

DESIGN CONSIDERATIONS

Chapters 4–8

## CHAPTER 4

THE NUTS AND BOLTS OF DESIGN

THE IMPORTANCE OF DESIGN

After reading Part 1 and discussing the results of the worksheets with your client, you will have learned how to identify your client's needs to plan their small home. Now you are ready to have some fun with design and put all of your ideas in effect. Design, after all, is planning many parts, putting them altogether and making a satisfying whole.

Often, clients think that interior designers only work for privileged, rich clients. Actually, professional interior designers find satisfaction and opportunities in designing for people with different needs. The American Society of Interior Designers has been at the forefront of sustainable design, design for aging, design for people with special needs, evidence-based design and design for health and wellness.

All people can use help with their home designs – especially within the constraints of small dwellings. Designers look for ways to make spaces function efficiently, look aesthetically pleasing, increase productivity and meet emotional satisfaction even when existing spaces don't always conform to smooth solutions.

Health, safety and welfare are professional goals, which are loaded with meaning. We want our homes to function properly and support productivity, but we also want them to be psychologically satisfying and stimulating. You, as an interior designer, possess a battery of strategies to develop unique spaces to reach your clients' goals.

This part of the book will review design theory, space planning and attention to human considerations as they relate to the design process when planning small dwellings. We will also look at specific small dwelling issues related to this design process in Part 3.

THE DESIGN PROCESS WHEN PLANNING SMALL DWELLINGS

The design process, typically, includes programming, concept development, schematic design, space planning, design development, documentation, administration tasks and post evaluation. The designer will be required to involve themselves with all or just some of these phases. Whether designing small or large, residential or commercial, the process is basically the same.

Because programming is central to our philosophy that participatory design is significant, we covered it at length in Part 1. Programming exercises were created to identify client needs, goals and facts, which can be analyzed and developed into a design concept. We will also cover programming exercises for specific small dwelling issues in Part 2 and Part 3.

It is important, early on, to create a well-developed design concept as your reference point. Design concepts are key ideas, formulated from understanding the client's needs and desires, the building or site, various constraints and other abstract influences that prompt emotional responses. For example, a client's interest in a piece of artwork or artist might drive the overall theme or idea of the design. Dodsworth and Anderson (2015, 38) explain,

... there is a need to find a unifying idea that will hold the disparate parts of the design together. This single idea will be one that sets the stylistic tone of the design. It is this single idea that is the concept.

From the programming phase, the designer explores design options during the schematic phase. Depending on the program information, the designer contemplates and communicates spatial possibilities, finishes, materials, furnishings, fixtures and equipment (FF&E). All the while, the client is an integral member of the team in deciding upon and approving room and furniture layout ideas, FF&E selection, and materials and finish choices. The designer will probably meet frequently with the client with sketches, drawings, samples and, possibly, models as the design becomes more and more refined.

Phases of design development, documentation and administration require revisions, review and finalization of all the many aspects of the design at hand. When designing a small home, the designer will have particular challenges and opportunities related to the constraints of space, size and square footage. Whether it is the layout of rooms and furnishings, storage space or the need for psychological spaciousness, the designer will need to draw upon design theory, planning knowledge and human factor information to help with the process.

In the following chapters we will discuss how design theory, space planning and attention to needs contribute to the design process and, ultimately, the health, safety and well-being of the client. You will uncover elements and principles of design theory for small dwellings, with an entire chapter on color and lighting. We also cover space planning and a further look at human interface attributes.

Dodsworth, Simon and Anderson (2015, 121) explain human interface as "the user's experience of the space – particularly the way that sight, touch, and sound define that experience ..." With that, we will cover building elements, finishes, FF&E, detailing and sustainable solutions.

PREFACE OF A CASE STUDY, *ARANUI 5*

In designing small dwellings, there is much to learn from designers who have tackled small quarter problems in nontraditional living environments. Ships, trains and mobiles have always been romanticized and seductive, but can also teach us how to design tight spaces.

Whether grounded or afloat, the design team has to analyze a program and formulate a responsive design concept. Team 7 International, based in San Francisco, California drew upon design theory, planning knowledge and human factor information to complete the interior design of a sailing vessel. The designers contemplated spatial possibilities, finishes, materiality, furnishings, fixtures and equipment. They had to lay out rooms and furnishings, create storage space and analyze psychological spaciousness, just like any other small dwelling "on ground." Revisions, review and finalization were particularly ongoing in this project.

Aranui 5 succinctly illustrates a case study about developing a small living space design. The design process required accommodating needs ranging from functionality and aesthetics to undeniable issues of safety compliances to cultural dynamics. Team 7

Figure 4.1. Case Study Aranui 5.

Source: *Aranui 5,*Team 7 International.

International, under the leadership of Jack Tam, Principal Architect, was approached to design a sailing vessel that would combine passenger and freighter accommodations for a 14-day journey through Tahiti and the Marquesas Islands in the South Pacific.

CASE STUDY 4: *ARANUI 5*, TEAM 7 INTERNATIONAL, JACK TAM PRINCIPAL ARCHITECT AND ANDREW TANG DESIGNER, SAN FRANCISCO, CALIFORNIA, USA, 2013

The *Aranui 5* continues a long-standing tradition of providing unique, luxurious and adventurous travel between Tahiti and the Marquesas Islands: some of the most remote, unspoiled and breath-taking islands in the world. The ship combines passenger and freighter functions in one vessel, providing comfortable and safe accommodations for a 14-day journey through the Marquesas, where Herman Melville and Paul Gauguin landed and flourished.

Aranui 5 contains eight one-bedroom suites, 24 executive suites, 37 deluxe cabins and 50 standard cabins. The ship's amenities include restaurants, lounges, spa, exercise gym, beauty parlor, a shopping center, a computer center, a photo studio and conference facilities. The ship has fully encased twin engines ensuring reliability and safety at sea.

Team 7 International subtly interjected local cultural elements into the overall design. Tattoo motifs, incorporated in screens and furnishing patterns, immerse passengers into a Tahitian environment. Colors and patterns resonate with tropical natural environs and energize the space. Spatial organization has been thoroughly considered to provide versatile space for social gathering and accommodate inhabitants' needs.

Figure 4.2. Concierge Service Center for Aranui 5.

Source: *Aranui 5*, Team 7 International.

Figure 4.3. Many cultures are reflected in this project.

Source: *Aranui 5*, Team 7 International.

Interview: Jack Tam, Principal Architect, and Andrew Tang, Designer

How did you approach a global view of the design while working with different social, cultural and geographical backgrounds in this project?

A former Tahitian client asked us to consider designing a passenger vessel that would sail through the Marquesas in the South Pacific. Each island has distinct cultural differences. The ship was designed in Europe, but built in China. Many of the *Aranui 5* passengers are from Europe. So from the beginning of the project we had to consider a wide range of countries and cultures.

As we developed the design we kept each culture in mind. We tried many schematics and finally conceptualized the overall idea of using natural, tropical schemes.

Figure 4.4. Carved wood screens with tattoo images create a sense of privacy and delineation.

Source: *Aranui 5*,Team 7 International.

Cultural tattoo patterns are evident in screens and borders in the living quarters as well as natural, tropical colors and patterns. How did this concept come about and did you have any initial problems with this aesthetic? How did the ship's guests ultimately respond to the theme?

In the early stages of presenting ideas we realized that tattoo symbols on our brochure were not typical of all of the islands. The symbols were meaningful to Fijians but not to Tahitians. We had to be careful when selecting tattoo motifs. We designed carved wood screens with tattoo images, which created a sense of privacy and delineation.

The European guests seemed to like the overall aesthetic and didn't seem to mind the lower ceiling heights. We were concerned about the physicality of the taller European passengers.

What did you immediately learn about designing the interiors of a ship that ultimately influenced design development and planning?

We soon learned that we had to comply with a rigorous code, the Marine Equipment Directives (MED), under French jurisdiction, that has to do with the safety and quality of marine equipment of the ship. Every aspect of selecting interior elements was affected by this code.

When you are on water, unlike land, you need to be concerned about keeping structures, panels, built-ins and furnishings light in weight and balanced to keep the vessel afloat. Materiality has to pass stringent fire tests because there is basically no place to go when on water.

Figure 4.5. Lightweight locking panels meet unique marine code requirements.

Source: *Aranui 5,*Team 7 International.

We learned a great deal about lightweight locking panels that were made with an acoustical core, a sheared steel plate surface and a colored, textured veneer. We used other lightweight solutions, such as the carved wood screens in the cabins.

Other design considerations included incorporating curved corners on cabinetry and railings on edges of flat surfaces because of nautical rocking. Anything that moved freely such as hanging light fixtures had to be scrutinized for movement of the ship. Ceiling heights were a concern as they could only be seven feet or approximately 2.1 meters maximum. We tried various ceiling treatments but had to stay within the height limitation.

What were the dimensions of the cabins and what functional appointments were considered?

Figure 4.6. Louvered doors solve the weight problem and add texture and airiness to the space.

Source: *Aranui 5*,Team 7 International.

The cabins had to be carefully space-planned because of balance issues. The cabins ranged from the largest cabin, the Owner's Suite, at 30 square meters in size (322.92 square feet) to the smallest cabin at 13 square meters (139.93 square feet). Some rooms comprised luxury beds or bunk beds, cabinets for belongs, small refrigerators, tables, places for luggage and small bathrooms. Louvered doors solved the weight problem and added texture and airiness to the space. Depth of cabinetry was a consideration so we kept depths narrow and reconfigured storage. For example, hanging clothes were placed on a hanging rod that was perpendicular to the back wall.

We designed multipurpose furniture, such as tables that functioned for eating, writing and grooming. The lower portion of the tables accommodated mini refrigerators. We also utilized the underside of beds for luggage storage.

We incorporated faux synthetic rattan furnishings that were lightweight and carried through the tropical theme. We also used these simulated rattan veneers on drawer surfaces.

We used a variety of textures, light and bright colors to make the rooms feel spacious. Because we had to adhere to fire-resistant materials, we applied simulated wood veneers to wall panels, which carried through a natural look.

REFERENCES

American Society of Interior Designers. www.asid.org/.

Dodsworth, Simon and Stephen Anderson, 2015. *The Fundamentals of Interior Design*, 2nd ed. London: Fairchild Books.

## CHAPTER 5

ELEMENTS AND PRINCIPLES OF DESIGN FOR SMALL DWELLINGS

THE LANGUAGE OF DESIGN: ELEMENTS AND PRINCIPLES

Visual characteristics form the vocabulary that we refer to as elements and principles of design. Elements are parts of the design. Principles are guidelines in putting the parts or elements together to form a satisfying unit. In nature we observe similar examples of elements coming together to make an attractive whole. If you have some understanding of how the elements work you can manipulate them to create the environments that you want. This knowledge is particularly important in designing small spaces so that you can achieve spaciousness, emotional satisfaction and interest.

Elements of Design

Line
Form and shape
Space
Texture and pattern
Color – value, tint, shade, intensity, neutrals
Light

Principles of Design

Unity and harmony
Repetition and rhythm
Movement
Balance
Variety
Contrast
Emphasis/accent
Proportion and scale

OBSERVING DESIGN IN NATURE

The following exercise illustrates the interaction between elements and principles of design, which creates a means of expression. In *Observing Design in Nature* you will utilize and imitate nature to find creative ideas for your designs. The exercise was inspired by Benyus' (1997) book, *Biomimicry: Innovation Inspired by Nature.*

Take a walk, sit in nature or gaze out of a window. This is a nice way to open your eyes to design in nature and will help you identify the parts and characteristics of design. It is also a wonderful excuse to just enjoy nature and relax. I like to do this exercise as part of my daily walk, which doubles as a form of meditation. Take your sketchbook and a pencil so that you can record what you see. Worksheets are in Appendix A.

Figure 5.1. A winter morning scene in Montana.

Source: S. Halbe, Ann Ledon.

Observing Design in Nature Exercise Example

I am attracted to a winter morning scene from my window. I can use this color palette for my client who desires blue for her bedroom, but doesn't want it to appear too cold. This scene illustrates warmth of the ground colors with a variety of blue and pink tints and shades from the sky and the background trees.

OBSERVING DESIGN IN NATURE EXERCISE

Design is all around us. Observe nature and only think of what you see. Tune into your other senses. How does the experience make you feel? Keep other thoughts on hold while you only utilize your eyes, ears, nose, skin and movement of your body.

For example, let's say that you are walking down a path in Golden Gate Park in San Francisco. The exotic ferns are tall and feathery. The path twists and turns through a mini forest of dense greenery. You look ahead to a small grove of trees that bend over a pond. There is something about the light filtering through the tree tops that catches your eye. Stop and really observe what it is that attracts your attention. Take note of the colors that you see; different shapes in space; linear features such as the way branches intertwine; textures and patterns of the leaves; spaces of the sky in between branch shapes; and effects of the filtered light. Are the elements that you see balanced and in equilibrium? Does your eye move effortlessly from branch to branch with the repetition of linear movement? Are the elements harmonious and similar in color, lines or shapes? Is there a focal point or a dash of color here and there that attracts your attention; perhaps a jolt of a bright red blossom against the green leaves? Are there other contrasting colors, shapes and sizes?

How does an experience such as this make you feel? Does a tree scene feel lyrical and joyful or haunting and creepy? Take note of your responses. Does the space have aesthetic qualities? Can you figure out what makes it beautiful or not?

Figure 5.2. Pay attention to natural environments.

Source: S. Gannon.

By paying attention to natural environments you can understand human preferences for certain ways color, light, shape, line and other elements go together. How does your experience translate to what you want in an environment – comfort, shelter, stimulation, etc.? How can you incorporate natural elements and principles into your design? How could you apply color blends, light patterns, focal points and overall light in your interior that would satisfy your environmental needs?

If your client prefers modern, simple lines, what can you learn from observing vertical, slender tree branches with clean edges and interesting negative spaces?

Figure 5.3. Look for depth and drama in nature.

Source: S. Gannon.

Does the scene feel dramatic and directional? What other aesthetic, metaphorical or functional aspects of nature could you mimic in a design?

Sketch, photograph and take notes about what you experience in nature and what innovations or thoughts come to mind. Share your experience with a friend to help articulate your observations and feelings. Enjoy your experience.

We will further discuss how nature affects us in Chapter 8, "Tapping Nature and Sustainability for Solutions." We will also look at the concept of biophilia. Edward O. Wilson defined biophilia as the human "... urge to affiliate with other forms of life," (Kellert and Wilson 1995, 416).

Remember that when you arrange and plan a design you can draw upon some of the lessons that nature teaches us. You want to be aware of creating a home that is harmonious with related elements and eye movement, but you also want it to have contrast and variety. Because an interior is three-dimensional, you need to become aware of how shapes (furniture, accessories, fixtures, etc.) look in space. Are they pleasing in proportion and scale and are they balanced – either symmetrically or asymmetrically?

Utilizing elements and principles of design can help you offset constraints of space and size that are inherent in small dwellings. Next we will review each element and principle of design and how you can use them when designing small.

WHAT EACH PRINCIPLE CAN DO FOR YOU

Unity and Harmony

Unity is the quality of all of the parts working together as a whole. Harmony is the pleasing agreement of similar parts such as common shapes, sizes and materials. When designing small dwellings we want the eye to travel effortlessly around the room.

Repetition, Rhythm, Movement and Balance

Rhythm is the visual repetition of regular spacing and elements such as lines or color in a composition. Repetition creates visual direction and movement, which also contributes to the unity of the composition. We find satisfaction when we can easily explore an interior by looking from one item of furniture or accessory to the next. If our eyes are transfixed by a grouping of furniture with no other visual place to go, we often feel unconsciously bothered. We are curious creatures and like to look around. Balancing furnishings and color are also important because we as humans like visual equilibrium. An arrangement may be symmetrical or asymmetric, but it needs to balance out with "heavier" or "lighter" colors, shapes, etc.

Figure 5.4. Symmetrical balance can be used in a small living room.

Source: C. Barry.

Variety, Contrast and Emphasis

Variety provides us a change when elements are too similar. Contrast and emphasis give us a visual bolt that assists with exploration of the whole design and engagement. You can achieve contrast by mixing darkness and lightness, different colors, small and large shapes and different textures, from smooth to rough.

Proportion and Scale

Proportion is the visual relationship of one part to another. We humans tend to be drawn to the visuals that relate in magnitude and in quantity. If we hang a picture on the wall, for example, we not only consider the size of the picture but the relationship of the picture to the wall space behind the picture. We like groupings of pictures that are balanced and placed in such a way that the wall space

Figure 5.5. Variety gives us the feeling of tension that we enjoy when elements are too similar.

Source: Sherrill Baldwin Halbe Interior Design, S. Halbe.

Figure 5.6. These furnishings are in relative proportion to the client's size.

Source: Sherrill Baldwin Halbe Interior Design, Mark Lund Photography.

is pleasing, contributing to the unity and movement of the entire interior. Ancient Greeks understood this relationship and termed it the Golden Section.

People also tend to prefer the scale or the size of an item to be relative to their size and scale. Proper scale serves us both visually and functionally; for example, being able to reach a cabinet shelf. We find satisfaction when furniture and other household items are in relative proportion to our size.

PRACTICAL APPLICATIONS OF ELEMENTS AND PRINCIPLES

Depending on the size and shape of a room you can use elements to your advantage to create the look and emotion that you want. We will continue this discussion later on when we illustrate Rose's condo design and explain how we manipulated the space to her liking.

Lines at Work

Lines have a sense of direction and affect our perception of space. Horizontal lines seem restful, low and stable. Vertical lines express strength, upward movement and height. Diagonal lines have definite movement and are often dramatic. Depending on the furnishing and the color, thin lines may seem lyrical and heavier lines, solid. You can create rhythm and order with lines. If you need the illusion of widening a room you can apply furnishings that have a horizontal linear look. Choosing a sofa that is low and long with an accompanying chair can achieve this goal.

Figure 5.7. If a form or plane feels too solid you can use materials that convey transparency such as these doors.

Source: C. Barry.

Forms and Shapes at Work

Furnishings can psychologically achieve feelings of stability. Shapes and forms are part of the room's composition that can either add movement or divert too much visual motion. Squares and some rectangular shapes can feel stable, whereas curved spaces may seem carefree or intriguing. Other elements like a series of sofa pillows against the background of a sofa can add repetition and contrast. If a form or plane feels too solid you can use material that conveys transparency, such as kitchen and closet fronts or transparent doors.

Figure 5.8. This home office demonstrates spatial interest and eye movement with the placement of artwork and furnishings.

Source: Michael Hospelt Photography, WEISBACH architecture | design, Gar Rector and Associates.

Space at Work

Importantly, the space behind shapes needs to be just as balanced, harmonious and interesting as the shapes in front of it. You can give space interest and eye movement by arranging furniture so that it forms a silhouette against a wall – the negative space – and the wall will take on a shape of its own. Squint your eyes and examine a wall behind a sofa. Does the space have interesting eye movement and attractive proportion?

Rose's discovery of placing kitchen dishes in a stark white cabinet in Chapter 11 is a great example of this. To her delight, she noticed that the white backdrop of the cupboards and shelves provided a perfect frame and negative space for her multicolored bowls and plates. The white background not only helped emphasize the col-ored shapes of the dishes, but formed a contrasting negative space with charming liveliness and unique character.

Textures and Patterns at Work

Textures and patterns are the surface quality of form. Lines, colors and shapes can make up the visual or tactile feel of textures and patterns. They can feel smooth or rough and heavy or light. You can determine what mood or optical illusion you want and then choose fabrics, furniture and so forth to reach your goals.

Color and Light at Work

We will discuss all of the elements' attributes as you read on; but first a word on color. Color takes on rank because it can come to our rescue in so many ways. Like the thrill a kid has when she opens a new box of crayons, color is exciting and delicious with so many

Figure 5.9. Textures from nature can inspire our designs.

Source: S. Halbe.

Figure 5.10. Lines, colors and shapes can make up the visual or tactile feel of textures and patterns.

Source: C. Barry.

hues to choose from. The next chapter will talk about color and light and what it can do for us.

CASE STUDY 5: LITTLE HOUSE ON THE PRAIRIE, SHERRILL BALDWIN HALBE INTERIOR DESIGN, GREAT FALLS, MONTANA, USA, 2015

Little House on the Prairie is a 750 square feet (69.68 square meters) house, located in the center of Montana, a prairie setting surrounded by the Rocky Mountains. Family members who individually live all over the world and occasionally come back to their home town inherited the 80-year-old house. The new owners expressed multifunctional goals of upgrading the house on a limited budget and eventually selling it. In the meantime, they wanted to use it as a

Figure 5.11. A vignette in Little House on the Prairie.

Source: Sherrill Baldwin Halbe Interior Design.

guesthouse. Above all, the family wanted to keep the integrity of the house and the emotional feel of their past home.

This account illustrates how a Program bridged the process of recognizing the clients' needs and applying design theory to meet their needs. With careful listening and programming techniques, Sherrill helped her clients identify their needs and experiences and plan for the family's special requirements and remodeling goals. The resulting design reflects the story and the heart of the clients' wishes.

Interview: Sherrill Baldwin Halbe

How did you begin the programming process?

I was involved with an interior plan for the little house that had seen many years on the Montana prairie but was recently surrounded by contemporary homes. The clients' described their family home as belonging to their mother, a sweet, dear lady who lived her entire life there and kept it cozy and warm with her presence and good cooking.

First of all, I went through a process of finding out what they wanted, what existed in the house, what the family could afford and their future plans. When I interviewed the adult children they said that they would eventually sell the house, but in the meantime, stay in the house when they visited the area. My job was to update the house, make it appear breezy and spacious and retain the essence of their mother. They wanted me to come up with an interior plan that would accommodate visitors, but also appeal to the open market for future sale.

Figure 5.12. The clients' memories and impressions of their mother inspired this design.

Source: Sherrill Baldwin Halbe Interior Design.

I found inspiration for the design from stories about their mother and a few found items in the house. A collectible green teapot, a few old green-handled kitchen utensils and a tea towel told the story of this little house that was built in the 1930s.

After interviewing the clients, what were the main ideas that drove the design concept?

Toby Israel (2010) in *Some Place Like Home: Using Design Psychology to Create Ideal Places* believes in uncovering memories and impressions of places to reveal a sense of home. The clients' memories of their mother's cooking and cozy shared times at family meals brought up the warmth of this home where simple family values were abundant.

The kitchen was the heart of this house. The clients wanted to keep the spirit of their mother's home so I started with the kitchen where I imagined the aroma of fresh bread and roasted meats still lingered. Inspired by the kitchen collectibles, I chose similar colors and styles.

What other design solutions did you choose based on these ideas?

We transformed the walls from a bright yellow, which was typical of her day, to a light Benjamin Moore Hollingsworth Green paint. The adjacent space of the living room carried through with a custom color that I call Eggnog, which is very close in intensity. By painting large 1 × 3 feet (.30 × .91 meters) sample boards in these colors, I observed the colors in the light at different times of the day to see if the color palette would work.

Figure 5.13. Green knick-knack shelves show off a green teapot and other treasures.

Source: Sherrill Baldwin Halbe Interior Design.

One of the main design constraints was that the house was very small. How did you address color choices to give the illusion of spaciousness?

We cleaned, sanded and painted the existing dark-stained kitchen cupboards with Benjamin Moore Linen White. I chose washable wallpaper as a backsplash, which was similar in color as the walls but added some small texture. Glass cabinet knobs in various green colors and tints added playfulness and eye movement to the otherwise monochromatic scheme. Knick-knack shelves held green teapots and other treasures that their mother had.

Adjacent areas in smaller spaces do well with similar colors, lightness and pureness of color. Continuity from one area to another gives the feeling of connectedness. I also considered the exterior paint and the surroundings of the house. Research has shown it is not the color that matters as much as the intensity of the color. Brighter (pure) colors appear closer than duller colors (colors that have been neutralized with other colors or neutrals). Another thing to watch for is contrasts in brightness of adjacent colors, which advance and create spatial tightness. I used similar colors throughout.

What were some of the space planning advantages?

There were existing arched passageways from kitchen to living room and a hallway to the bedrooms, which provided transparency of

Figure 5.14. Adjacent areas in smaller spaces do well with similar colors, lightness and pureness of color. Continuity from one area to another gives the feeling of connectedness.

Source: Sherrill Baldwin Halbe Interior Design.

Figure 5.15. Morning light was allowed to stream into the kitchen from a window that looked onto a garden space.

Source: Sherrill Baldwin Halbe Interior Design.

seeing one space to another. This provided a spatial illusion of continuity and connectedness in each room.

Another way to obtain transparency is to create an indoor–outdoor look with windows and transparent doors to decks or gardens.

Speaking of windows, what other lighting solutions did you implement?

I selected window treatment that was neutral and simple, allowing as much natural light in as possible. I permitted morning light to stream into the kitchen from an east window that looked onto a garden space. The clients will consider flower boxes affixed to the exterior of the window to add connectivity to the outdoors.

I considered ambient, task and accent lighting sources for a variety of aesthetic and functional illumination. Dark spaces appear smaller

and can be confining. I used indirect lighting and lamps for their warm glow and spatial depth.

What other design tricks did you use to make the interiors seem expansive?

A space tends to feel smaller and is perceived as a whole if a uniform color is used exclusively in all rooms, without some variety and balance. I planned similar but different colors in various rooms and in accessories and materials.

Figure 5.16. Collectible mirrors, in various shapes, were placed here and there for reflection and the illusion of space, light and sparkle.

Source: Sherrill Baldwin Halbe Interior Design.

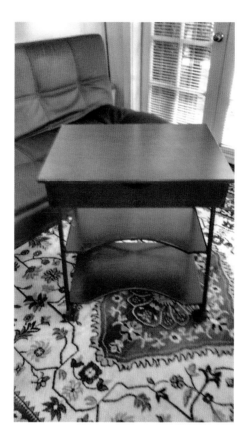

Figure 5.17. Multifunctional furnishings with casters work well for flexibility.

Source: Sherrill Baldwin Halbe Interior Design.

Simplicity in materials, textures, finishes, furnishings and acces-sories can provide a calm and relaxing space in a small area. Subtle variety can be achieved with various textures such as smooth and rough surfaces. I selected smaller prints and plain colored fabrics for furnishings. An analogous scheme (similar colors next to each other on the color wheel) such as greens, yellow greens and blue greens in various tints, neutrals and shades provide continuous eye movement and harmony. These color choices provide a serene place for the visiting family and visually enlarge the space.

There is a large mirror in the living room, which reflects outdoor light and views. Smaller, collectible mirrors, in various shapes, were placed here and there for the illusion of space, light and sparkle.

I chose scaled-down, multifunctional furnishings that could be used for storage and hiding clutter. I looked for furnishings that had raised legs with casters that would appear roomy and could be easily moved for family flexibility.

Lastly, I arranged memorabilia and functional small accessories, leaving some empty space to show off pieces and avoid clutter. To ground an already airy space, these vignettes added color and completed the small house design.

Did the resulting design satisfy the original design concepts?

Yes, especially the concept of keeping the family spirit alive in this little house. Doig (1973, 314) expressed it well in *This House of Sky: Landscapes of a Western Mind*. "I am left to think through the fortune of all we experienced together. And of how, now, my single outline meets the time-swept air that knew theirs."

REFERENCES

Benyus, Janine. 1997. *Biomimicry: Innovation Inspired by Nature.* New York, NY: HarperCollins Publishers Inc.

Doig, Ivan. 1973. *This House of Sky: Landscapes of a Western Mind.* New York, NY: Houghton Mifflin Harcourt Publishing Company. 314.

Israel, Toby. 2010. *Some Place Like Home: Using Design Psychology to Create Ideal Places.* Princeton, NJ: Design Psychology Press.

Kellert, Stephen R. and Edward O. Wilson. 1993. *Biophilia.* Washington, DC: Island Press. 416.

CHAPTER 6

COLOR AND LIGHT

Figure 6.1. Abundance of color and light is shown in this small bathroom.

Source: Hole Photography, B. and H. Hartsock, Gar Rector and Associates.

THE ABUNDANT COLOR OF BEING

Sometimes choosing colors for one's interior environment is an insufferable, confusing task for clients. There are many characteristics of color and it is hard to know what will work. There are numerous lighting variables; psychological, social, and cultural effects and preferences; ways that colors can be combined or placed next to each other to get different effects; interpretations of color weight, movement and temperature; and individual preferences vs. trends and styles. And to add to that, there are a gazillion colors to choose from, let alone the altered appearance of color in textures, patterns and metallic materials. Clients can be confused and frustrated when working alone. You can be a great help to clients in choosing colors.

All of these characteristics need to be addressed, but first let's look at preferences of color and how to help your client choose colors that are right for them. We will also look at color trends.

PREFERENCES OF COLOR AND TRENDS

We will talk about psychological, sociological and cultural preferences, but sometimes we just have individual associations and responses with color. For example, one might not want a yellow room simply because of the thought of a grandparent's kitchen. We might love our grandmother and her kitchen but want our own identity with colors.

Have your client check out their closet and see what they tend to wear or prefer. It may be different from what they think. Have them leaf through interior magazines and tear out photos of rooms that seem to attract them or look online. Have them keep a folder and after a while, help them look for similar patterns of color scheme choices.

Many times color preferences develop because of one's geographic area. Studies have shown that people in different countries not only have single color likes and dislikes but they prefer different combinations of colors or schemes. No matter what we prefer for whatever reason it is good to be aware of the power of trends and preferences of colors.

Color trends usually go through consumer phases of what is in style in clothing, paint, furniture and products to what is popular in cars. What is trendy today may be unappealing in another decade. Help your client identify colors that are preferred rather than what the latest market dictates.

We have included adventures and exercises in learning to "see" colors for your client. Read *Learning to See Exercises for Your*

Figure 6.2. This bureau shows whimsical use of color.

Source: C. Barry.

Client and then *A Color Exercise for a "Room of One's Own"* to help your client realize their favorites. There are worksheets for your client in Appendix A.

ADVENTURES AND EXERCISES IN LEARNING TO "SEE" COLORS

Invite your client on an adventure to "see" colors and learn how to recognize their affinity to colors. The first and most important aspect of color selection is to become acquainted with your client's personal color preference, not preferences necessarily driven by commercial trends and styles. Here are some exercises for your client to sharpen their awareness of color and color use.

Learning to See Exercises for Your Client

1. Look at color in nature. Take a walk or sit in the mountains or park and do nothing but walk or sit, enjoy the day and look at the subtleties of the tiniest and largest parts of nature. Take note of the color of soil, grasses, lights and darks of tree bark, varieties of shades and tints of green leaves, or filtered light and shade on rocky creeks. Observe nature that especially catches your eye and ask yourself why you are attracted. Is there interesting contrast, harmony, variety, movement, balance, proportion, or emphasis related with the colors? How does a specific observation make you feel? Journal your notes, sketches or photographs.

Figure 6.3. Observe nature. Are there principles of design at play? How can you apply these characteristics to an interior?

Source: S. Halbe.

2. Keep a folder of magazine photos or photographs of interiors that really, really attract you. Discuss why a particular part of the room in the photo stands out. Is it the color, the color combination, darks and lights or characteristics such as contrasts or variety? Write notes on the picture and save the ideas for future use.

3. Gather color samples of paint chips, fabric, tile, wood, etc. and keep a color collection of items you love. Make a color material board by gluing samples for a room on poster board. You might find the color in a sample of tile that could be made into paint. Your local paint store is usually very good at matching colors. Your designer can help you find samples.

Figure 6.4. This color selection was inspired by the Balenciaga and Spain exhibit.

Source: S. Halbe; Palais Royale, Mahogany and Abyssinian tile by Ann Sacks.

4. Keep your eye alert to visual advertisements of clothing, products and art that attract your attention. Visit art shows and keep visual records of pieces that inspire passion.

Here's an example of the latter. An exhibit at the de Young Fine Arts Museum in San Francisco exhibited a collection of fabulous fashion pieces from the designer, Balenciaga. His inspiration for this particular exhibition of clothing was drawn from his experiences in his native Spain. A hypothetical "room of one's own" creation could be inspired by Balenciaga's combinations of blacks and reds with sparks of jewel colors.

Enjoy the abundance of your colors.

A Color Exercise for a "Room of One's Own"

Help your client imagine a real room that they already have. The following exercises are written for the designer and the client.

Example

1. The first step is to really look at the materials and furnishings that will stay in the room. Everything has color with the exception of black, gray, and white and these neutrals are part of the color palette. Train your eye to see the black–red in brick, the blue–gray in stone, and the brownish-gold of wood flooring. Get samples, if you can and add them to a color material collection.

The flooring is wooden plank that has a gray brown look to it. I want to keep the dark brown

Figure 6.5. Natural light such as northern exposure or the filtering of light from outdoor foliage enhances indoor space. Remember views have color.

Source: S. Halbe.

leather settee and the rustic wood coffee table with metal legs.

2. Secondly, take note of the room's lighting sources such as windows and artificial lighting. Note the orientation of natural light such as northern exposure or the filtering of light from outdoor foliage or indoor window treatment. Do you have a view? Views have color.

The office room has southern and eastern exposure with French doors and operable windows. There are views of outdoor fields and the mountains. Seasonal colors are prevalent in this room. Presently there is a general lighting source on the ceiling and task lighting. Shades are needed when the sunlight is *too bright. With all of the available light, house plants grow readily.*

3. Next, note the areas of the room that will require color choices such as walls, floors, ceilings, trim, window treatment, doors, windows, built-ins, lighting fixtures and furnishings. Don't forget hardware such as door knobs and handles, accessories and artwork.

We will need to choose colors for the walls, floor, ceiling, trim, window treatment, doors, windows, lighting fixtures, desk and cabinetry.

Figure 6.6. This setting demonstrates colors and treasures gathered from the client's travels abroad.

Source: C. Barry.

4. Now, have some fun, and think about the kind of atmosphere you want to create in your room: Would it be a calm and restful room or stimulating and playful? Perhaps it is refined and dignified or just laid back. Write down the colors that might lend themselves to this atmosphere.

We want to create a sitting area that is lively and interesting. We want to display some of our treasures that we have collected during our travels.

PRIMER OF COLOR AND LIGHT GUIDELINES AND BREAKING THE RULES

We have included some of the characteristics and rules of color use so that you, the designer, can help the client manipulate color to their advantage in designing small dwellings. One rule, however, is that you consider these color guidelines and then think for yourself – be creative and try new ways. Break the rules. Rose was once told that she should stay away from wearing yellow tones because they made her look too yellow. I am here to tell you that she looked gorgeous on her wedding day wearing a beautiful turmeric yellow silk dress. I'm glad she did it her way.

It is helpful to remember how color perception works. The mechanics of seeing color involves multiple, complex ways we actually recognize and prefer colors. In a nutshell, we need to have light to see color – color is light; light is absorbed or reflected on surfaces or matter; we generally need to have sight to see color and we perceive color according to how our brains interpret each color – covering a whole gamut of psychological, sociological, cultural, individual, physical and perceptual forces at work.

Figure 6.7. Playful lighting can be seen from both the kitchen and living room.

Source: Hole Photography, B. and H. Hartsock, Gar Rector and Associates.

It is important for interior designers to stay current on research-based color and light studies. Good accounts on color and light are in research-based editions of *Color: The Secret Influence* by Dr. Kenneth R. Fehrman and Cherie Fehrman (2015).

Read on. Let's look at some interesting but sometimes problematic characteristics of color and light.

LIGHTING

Different types of daylight such as north and south, seasonal and regional light cast different colored light on different surfaces, which influence the final coloration. Light from a northern window

Figure 6.8. Lighting can be manipulated to achieve the mood and the spaciousness that you want.

Source: S. Gannon.

will cast a more bluish light on a surface than the yellowish light from a southern window. Other lighting sources, like incandescent lighting, LEDs and fluorescent lighting cast different colors on interior surfaces. For example, old-style fluorescent lighting appears greener than the warmer incandescent lighting. However, it is easier

Figure 6.9. Task lighting
under a kitchen cabinet
provides functional
illumination and a
soft mood.

Source: Sherrill Baldwin
Halbe Interior Design, L.
Barber.

these days to buy lighting sources with a coloration that you prefer. Always choose interior colors such as paint or fabric under the type of lighting that exists already or will be in the space.

Lighting can be manipulated to achieve the mood and the spaciousness that you want. Indirect lighting and lamps can provide a warm glow and spatial depth. Dark spaces appear smaller and confining and lighter areas feel expansive.

Remember, though, light can also create glare and reflection or be absorbed by some colors such as dark colors. These characteristics can be problematic if you need to avoid glare while using your computer or need greater light to see in darker surroundings. Older people have trouble with glare and reflective surfaces, but still need proper lighting to see efficiently.

Circadian lighting is a consideration for healthy buildings and a component of the WELL Building Standard. "Circadian lighting calls for a boost of blue-rich light during the daylight hours to help bolster the body's circadian rhythm" (Lee 2016, 18). Lee explains that warmer light is appropriate for evening and promotes melatonin, which regulates sleep (Lee 2016, 14–20).

A trick of the trade is to layer your lighting sources in an interior. For example, use ambient, general lighting for all-around vision; task lighting such as a desk light or lighting under a kitchen cabinet for certain jobs; and accent and decorative lighting such as chandeliers for sparkle and pendant lighting for pizzazz or as a focal point.

COLOR PERCEPTION AND EFFECTS

Colors Next to Other Colors

Colors look differently when they are next to any other color. For example, a red and white checker sofa will appear pink from a distance. Our eyes blend red and white just like a paint brush. The same goes for blue and red in a plaid. We perceive purple or violet. This knowledge can work to our advantage if that is what we want but to our disadvantage if we don't want pink or violet as part of our overall color scheme.

Figure 6.10. Uniformity of color increases the space with a variety of color of furnishings and accessories for eye movement.

Source: Gar Rector and Associates.

This phenomenon is called simultaneous contrast. Other adjacency occurrences are described by Merriam Webster as,

the tendency of a color to induce its opposite in hue, value and intensity upon an adjacent color and be mutually affected in return by the law of *simultaneous contrast* a light, dull red will make an adjacent dark, bright yellow seem darker, brighter and greener; in turn, the former will appear lighter, duller and bluer

"Light-reflecting colors emphasize space" (Fehrman and Fehrman, 2015, 111) and uniformity of color can increase the perception of space. However, they note that uniformity can have the converse effect if it is used exclusively in all rooms. In a small house, without

Figure 6.11. A setting of brownish orange leather chairs with dark blue pillows is an example of toning down complementary colors.

Source: S. Halbe, Sonoma Country Antiques.

some variety or eye movement, the space can be perceived as a whole and tends to feel smaller. A designer can perceptually make a space seem larger by using a variety of colors that are similar in value and intensity or, in reverse, similar colors with a variety of values. The designer can add variety by tweaking similar colors with adjacency blends in textures and patterns that are characteristic of draperies, wall coverings and furnishings. You can also use different colors in accessories and other finishes.

For "in your face" contrast, combine colors that are opposite on the color wheel (complementary colors) such as blue and orange. If this is what you want – enjoy! If you want to use these combinations but want softer versions, you can choose colors that are toned down with tints, shades or neutrals such as brownish orange leather chairs with dark blue pillows.

It is useful if you understand what happens when one color is next to another color. Use it to your advantage. Designers often use or avoid optical illusions, such as when you place something dark on a lighter surface it appears darker whereas a light color on a darker color seems lighter. Gray will appear warmer against a blue background (Pile, 2007, 326). Luster can be achieved by putting a bright color on a deep navy or a black background.

Temperature, Weight and Movement of Color

Colors create interesting perceptions of temperature and movement. We have heard that yellows and reds are warmer and blues and greens are cooler. Although color temperature is a psychological reaction, thermal comfort has been associated with these colors. As designers we can manipulate the overall plan by choosing warmer or cooler colors. We can also choose colors with warm or cool undertones. For example, we can use warmed-up gray paint with the addition of red and yellow. We can also manipulate warm or cool colors with adjacent colors that are their opposites. *Case Study 6: A Young Couple's Bedroom* illustrates the way gray walls were warmed up with undertones and warm furnishings and accessories.

Colors also appear to advance or recede, feel solid and grounded or give the impression of "floating." Some colors seem to be lighter or heavier.

Humans often associate hues and values by their experiences with the Earth. We sometimes feel grounded with dark flooring (as the ground), associate walls as being lighter as in nature and lighter yet with the ceiling (as the sky).

Yet, as aptly put by Fehrman and Fehrman, (2015, 98) regarding the perception of spaciousness,

... perception of spaciousness is not attributed to specific colors, but rather to the brightness or darkness of a color. Second, spatial impressions are highly influence by contrast effects, particularly brightness differences between objects and backgrounds.

With this knowledge you can maneuver space. For example, to avoid the feeling of being in an elevator in a small space with a high ceiling, you can paint the ceiling with a darker color and the room won't feel as tall. Lighter and brighter colors often appear larger and open. Darker colors seem smaller and intimate.

Caution: Remember this about color guidelines. Be creative. You can always counterbalance advancing effects with other furnishings and accessories that give eye movement and receding effects. You can manipulate colors to your advantage if you are aware of the ways colors are perceived and affect us.

PSYCHOLOGICAL, SOCIOLOGICAL AND CULTURAL ASPECTS OF COLOR

We have heard that colors have psychological, sociological and cultural meaning. Humans often associate hues and values by their experiences with the earth. Green might mean spring and freshness to one person but sick or evil to another. We all give different meaning to colors. Based on individual preferences, black may be classy to one person but depressing to another. We can figure out our own preferences and choose colors that we want. You can create moods in rooms by knowing what different colors do to you. Here's a simple exercise for your clients to find out how they interpret color.

Color Association Exercise for the Client

Write down the first thing you think about when you hear or read a name of a color. Don't think too long or hard – just the first thing that comes to mind. There is no right or wrong answer, but you will see how your response to a color might have psychological, sociological or cultural associations.

Example:

Red - Bright, hot, exciting
Green - fresh, spring, natural

Color Association Exercise for the Client

Red	Red–Orange
Blue	Blue–Green
Yellow	Yellow–Green
Violet	Red–Violet
Green	Black
White	Blue–Violet
Orange	Yellow–Orange
Gray	Brown

A designer should be aware of his clients' associations with colors. When there is more than one person in a household, the designer needs to know each person's color associations, so that he can help the clients make comfortable color choices. In a small house where space is limited, this is critical.

PHYSICAL CONSIDERATIONS

Many people have physical sight issues that are important to understand. An older person may have difficulty with glare and contrasts and may see colors differently as their eyes age. Colors may take on a yellow cast.

Defective color vision is more prevalent than we think and affects many people in different ways. Some people confuse color types whereas most people can see different colors with clarity. For example, red may be confused as yellow or green. Whether it be age or a type of defective color vision it is good to be aware of what your clients' families can see and choose your colors accordingly for less confusion and discomfort.

Other physical outcomes of color exposure are shown in various research studies. For example, pink rooms seem to calm prisoners when they are newly incarcerated. The effect subsides after a brief time and may not be a permanent fix, in case you know someone who could benefit from a calming environment.

Again, as designers we should stay current with color studies. Research changes all the time and some studies are not always scientific. However, it is important to be alert to new color studies that catch our attention. Color does affect us in many ways, even physically.

COLOR SCHEMES

Be aware of color schemes but then tweak the schemes with other values, intensities, tints and colors for richer results. In small dwellings this is important. Although color schemes provide harmony and unity to overall palettes, one needs contrast and variety for eye movement and manipulation of size and space. Be conscious of how colors flow from room to room. Aim for harmonious transitions.

Complementary	Two complementary (opposite) colors on the color wheel
Split-complementary	Three colors splitting the complementary
Analogous	Two or three colors adjacent on the color wheel
Dyad	Two colors that are two colors apart
Triad	Three colors equally spaced on the color wheel
Tetrad	Four or more colors on the color wheel
Monochromatic	One color with a variety of tonal and chromatic values
Monotone	One color with one tonal and chromatic value
Achromatic	Neutrals: Various white, black, gray or brown ranges

MISHMASH TIPS FROM COLOR EXPERTS TO SHARE WITH CLIENTS

See if the paint store has an 8 × 10 inch (20.32 cm × 25.4 cm) color swatch instead of the 1 inch (2.54 cm) sample.

Ask the paint store employees how bright a color is going to be when it is dry.

When you pick out a color of paint, buy a jar or a quart first and try it at the client's home in the spot where it will be used. Look at it at various times of day in light and shade. If you can't use the client's home use another space with similar lighting conditions or paint large boards or cardstock and analyze at the site.

Paint a sample on a 2 × 4 feet (.5 × .10 meters) section of wall or you can paint a large sample on a board.

Take fabric swatches to the paint store to get a better match.

Figure 6.12. Various greens complement this kitchen.

Source: S. Halbe, C. and G. Lindberg.

Figure 6.13. Pendant lighting demonstrates small amounts of preferred blue for emphasis in the kitchen.

Source: S. Halbe, R. Mark and L. Beresford.

Use the "swivel chair" method of checking out a paint sample. Twirl around and hold the sample up, looking at any light changes or color changes.

Greens are complex, ranging from yellow to blue undertones.
Go slowly. Use your samples.
Take a break when your eyes are too saturated as your eyes will compensate.
Encourage your client to live with a large paint sample for a few days and decide upon the color after walking into the room with new "eyes."
Don't be afraid to paint walls. If you mess up you can always repaint.

If your favorite color just won't work in a space, use a small amount of the color for emphasis, such as blue in a pendant light.
Check ceiling height and wall distance relationships.
If the ceiling height is twice the distance of the wall there is less reflection. Sometimes you want reflective attributes; sometimes you don't.
Also check large reflective surfaces such as flooring, furniture and ceiling.
Check corners for different intensities of color.
Sometimes corners appear darker.

Now we can look at how to put colors and the other elements to work in the next chapter, "The Devil is In the Details." We'll take information from Rose's interview and her condo Program and translate her needs into a spatial and design plan.

Figure 6.14. A young couple's bedroom.

Source: Gar Rector and Associates, Hole Photography.

CASE STUDY 6: A YOUNG COUPLE'S BEDROOM, HOMEOWNERS SARAH AND GAR RECTOR, GAR RECTOR AND ASSOCIATES CONSTRUCTION, SAINT HELENA, CALIFORNIA, USA, 2016

Sarah and Gar Rector designed a master bedroom that meets their aesthetic preferences and doubles as a retreat. They live with their

twin five-year-olds in a 1200 square feet (111.48 square meters) house that backs up to a sloping hill in the Napa Valley of California overlooking vineyards. The only available space for the bedroom was on the first floor, which also houses the furnace and utilities. Physical constraints of the room dictated the space plan of the bedroom and natural light was limited. The young couple wanted a palette of color that would make a statement, but conform to the small area.

Figure 6.15. Warm grays can give the appearance of bluish tones.

Source: Gar Rector and Associates, Hole Photography.

You chose wonderful, subtle grays in your bedroom. Was it a choice of preference or did you have other reasons?

S:I've always preferred blue, but I was hesitant because of the size, shape and location of the bedroom. Natural light was limited with two small windows. We decided to make a statement by using warm

Figure 6.16. These west windows allow natural light for a long period of the day.

Source: Gar Rector and Associates, Hole Photography.

grays, which give the appearance of bluish accents and work with the constraints. We experimented with different neutrals and finally found a combination of grays with warmer undertones. We loved the color so much that we decided to use a light Pelican Gray by Benjamin Moore on the walls and a darker version on the custom cabinets in a semi-glossy sheen. We painted the custom coffered ceiling with the same paint, Silent Night, as the cabinets and the molding in a warm White Dove. Although it is a tight space the ceiling, trim and furnishings help the eye visually move around the room.

How did you make the bedroom feel light and airy without a lot of natural light?

G:We installed a French door that is adjacent to a well-lit entry allowing natural light in during the day. We installed several light

Figure 6.17. This bathroom was painted a very bright white which helps reflect light.

Source: Gar Rector and Associates, Hole Photography.

sources and a chandelier that gives the room sparkle. Our west windows allow natural light over a longer period of time and we don't cover the windows. We also get some natural light from the adjacent east master bathroom. The bathroom was painted a very bright white, which helps reflect light.

Figure 6.18. Lighting and yellow tones warm up the cool gray walls.

Source: Gar Rector and Associates, Hole Photography.

The room has a warm feel even though we often relate grays and blues with being cool. How did you get this effect?

S:Although we wanted the gray color throughout the bedroom, we chose a warm-colored carpet to counteract the coolness. I also

Figure 6.19. The same colored paint on the ceiling has the illusion of being lighter than the vertical cabinets.

Source: Gar Rector and Associates, Hole Photography.

Figure 6.20. The ins and outs of the coffered ceiling help break up the space and makes the ceiling feel higher.

Source: Gar Rector and Associates, Hole Photography.

placed warm yellow and orange artwork on both sides of the bed. Your eye is drawn up from the soft flooring to the walls. In addition, the paint has warm undertones with a bit of yellow ochre and red in the mixture.

You told me that you had to experiment with different shades for the ceiling paint to get the correct look that you wanted. Tell me about that.

G:The paint, Silent Night, on the horizontal ceiling plane had the illusion of being lighter than the vertical cabinets and actually looked like a different color. We had to paint different shades of the same color to get a consistent color similar to the cabinets. We

Figure 6.21. Depending on the light source at different times of day, the cabinetry color is never static.

Source: Gar Rector and Associates, Hole Photography.

Figure 6.22. The darker lower cabinets add drama to the white bathroom.

Source: Gar Rector and Associates, Hole Photography.

used a glossy paint on the cabinetry for more reflection of light, which livens up the darker color.

The ceiling really works aesthetically. Were there other reasons for incorporating the coffered ceiling?

S:We wanted to have gray throughout. The ins and outs of the coffered ceiling helps break up the space and makes the ceiling feel higher with its shades and reflections.

It is interesting that the cabinet colors look different in different types of light.

G:Yes, we like the idea of different colors depending on the light source at different times of day. It is never static.

REFERENCES

Fehrman, Kenneth R. and Cherie Fehrman. 2015. *Color: The Secret Influence*, 3rd ed. www.amazon.com/Color-Influence-Dr-Kenneth-Fehrman/ dp/0984200177/ref=sr_1_2?ie=UTF8&qid=1452042641&sr=8-2&keywo rds=Color%3A+The+Secret+Influence.

Lee, Lydia. 2016. "Tech Talk: Circadian Lighting." *ASID ICON* (Fall). 14–20.

Merriam Webster. Accessed August 3, 2017. www.merriamwebster.com/ dictionary/simultaneous%20 Contrast.

Pile, John F. 2007. *Interior Design*. Upper Saddle, NJ: Pearson Education, Inc.

CHAPTER 7

THE DEVIL IS IN THE DETAILS

SPACE PLANNING

After, programming and identifying what the client wants it is time to analyze need assessments and explore design development solutions. Look over your client's program and existing furnishings, equipment and fixtures (FF&E) to decide how to arrange their belongings. Think about what goes on in each area. People move through a space and travel from one room to another. They settle in places within their home to do tasks or relax and sleep in other places. As a designer, get to know your clients' habits so you can place the FF&E where needed.

It is also time to establish a design concept. As you recall, a design concept is a unifying idea that is formulated from understanding the client's needs and desires, the building or site, various constraints and other abstract influences that prompt emotional responses. From here you can start planning the space.

Higgins (2015, 7) explains space planning,

... it should be thought of as a truly three-dimensional challenge that involves considering: volume and form; the proportion, proximity and relationship of spaces; and the way in which they are articulated, defined and connected as well as the circulation between, through and around them. All of these elements have to be developed while managing to satisfy the needs of the interior's users and responding to the constraints established by the existing space in which the interior scheme is to reside.

Read *A Space Planning Checklist* first and keep each item in mind. Then start your plan by doing adjacency studies and diagraming.

Even in a small space a designer can draw area bubble diagrams to show zones of activities and their relationship to each other. Overlaying diagrams on tracing paper with hierarchical lines, arrows, notation and symbols help you solve problems with circulation, obstacles, views and focal points. Mandatory and secondary areas can be determined. Always refer back to *A Space Planning Checklist* during and at the end of the planning phase. Worksheets are in Appendix A.

A Space Planning Checklist

1. At the entrance have you provided enough space for physical movement and psychological transition from the outside of the home to the inside of the home?
2. Is there an inviting view within the area? Is there an interesting visual focal point from the entrance?

Figure 7.1. Two small windows add light, air and outside color to the kitchen.

Source: Hole Photography, B. and H. Hartsock, Gar Rector and Associates.

3. Check out window light and views and consider which rooms would benefit or not from light, heat and outside vistas.

4. In regard to building structure are there potential obstacles in room shapes and details? For example, are there long rectangular rooms, high or low ceilings, posts or narrow hallways?

5. Public and private areas – figure out ways to screen and accommodate personal areas from group areas.

6. Workable space – figure out the best place where the kitchen, bathroom, living room, etc. will function.

7. Are there areas that need to be next to each other? Place areas convenient to one another such as the eating area close to the kitchen or the bathroom near the bedroom.

Figure 7.2. Clear uncluttered space is used for easy movement within and outside of the seating area.

Source: W. and D. Hiebert, L. Barber.

8. Circulation within the spaces – provide enough space for physical movement and psychological transition from one space to another.

9. Furniture layout – think about spaces for entertainment; number of family members and their activities.

10. Circulation within seating areas – provide enough space for movement, sitting down comfortably and traffic paths within and outside of the seating area.

11. Sounds and smells – consider acoustical and odor challenges or opportunities from the outside and within.

HOW TO PUT IT ALL TOGETHER

To achieve the feeling of spaciousness, aesthetics and ease of function we can use color schemes, lighting, furnishings, fixtures, equipment, accessories and space planning techniques. We illustrate these techniques by showing you how we pulled Rose's condominium design together.

Architectural details also bring the design together. Detailing examples range from small construction elements such as molding and base trim to larger types of paneling and millwork. Details provide positive attributes in a small environment because of their qualities of transition, connection, function and enhancement of the overall design. In short, detailing can add eye movement, balance, variety, emphasis and contrast.

Designing Rose's Condo

We thought it would be helpful if we actually demonstrated, in part, how and what we came up with for a detailed plan for Rose's condo. Using all of the information from her interview, program surveys and our knowledge from space planning diagrams and checklists, we felt ready to put the puzzle together and figure out the design.

The design concept was at the forefront of the process, to create a place to cook, entertain and indulge in artistic and intellectual endeavors. The design incorporates custom and multifunctional furnishings that enhance functionality; spatial and color solutions that address human interface and factors; and basic function and aesthetics particular to Rose and Larry's needs.

Design Statement

Rose and Larry are owners of a 624 square feet (57.97 square meters) condominium at Phoenix Commons, a LEED-certified cohousing building for middle-aged and older residents. The units are individually owned and include shared ownership interest in common spaces. The common areas are comprised of a community room, a kitchen dining area, fitness and exercise room spaces and meeting rooms. The building was designed with features for aging in place. Rose and Larry were in charge of designing their own one bedroom and bathroom living quarters.

Rose and Larry are active, curious, professional writers who like to entertain, cook, read, walk the dog, listen to music, watch movies and enjoy community life. The couple wanted an interior that would accommodate and mirror their lifestyles and personalities. Rose explained, "I want my living environment to reflect who I am as well as meet my physical needs/limitations for now and the future. I'm on a fixed income with a small budget for home improvement and I want to use as much of what I already have rather than purchase new furniture."

This condominium design incorporates aesthetics and multifunctional ideas to house the owners' needs and requirements. Color schemes, lighting, furnishings, accessories and space planning techniques contribute to the feeling of spaciousness and ease of function.

Objectives

We designed the condo with the following objectives in mind:

> **To incorporate three prominent requirements: space and housing for cooking, entertaining and artistic endeavors – reading, writing and listening to music**
> **To make the condo space reflect Rose and Larry's lifestyle – welcoming, comfortable and spacious**
> **To utilize every square inch of space within the condo to satisfy all of Rose and Larry's activities, needs and desires**

Our first goal was to design for functionality, flexibility and adjustability. We did this by establishing multiple-use ideas to give the illusion of airiness. At the same time, we wanted to reflect a lively, intellectual atmosphere that was important to Rose and Larry's day-to-day life.

DESIGNING ROSE'S CONDO: A WALK THROUGH THE ENTRANCE

Condo Entry

Rose and Larry acquired a unit with a separate outdoor walkway leading to their entrance. The walkway is wide enough to provide a small patio area near the entrance door. A café-style patio table and chairs provide seating for alfresco dining as well as a place to view the peaceful estuary and shorebirds. A ceramic Chinese barrel stool provides additional seating for trimming plants or a drop in guest.

The two great cooks can pluck sprigs of rosemary or other herbs for their sauces from their potted garden area. The view from the kitchen connects them to their garden where fragrant flowers and a dwarf lemon tree provide a connection to nature.

Figure 7.3. Colors of outdoor plants and planters pave transition to indoor colors and objects.

Source: K. Turcznski.

As a transition from outside to inside, Rose chose outdoor furniture and planter pots that tied the outside colors to the interior color scheme. Rose and Larry are able to enjoy the varied colors of greenery and blooms from the inside window and the exterior entrance provides a cheery, welcoming connection to the interior.

Interior Entry

When guests or Rose and Larry enter the condo they need enough physical space to greet one another and take off their wraps. Given the scarcity of floor space, Rose chose to hang decorative hooks on the wall next to the front door instead of a standing coat rack. Hanging coats from one hook serves the additional function of hiding an electrical panel, which is painted the same color as the kitchen walls, Guilford Green. A second hook holds their dog's leash while various hats for Larry hang from the third hook. A two-sectioned receptacle keeps items for recycling, doggie bags and supplies neat and out of the way.

Rose and I found a patterned slip-free space rug for the entry area to serve as a decorative addition and for protecting the flooring beneath. This area rug provides a visual designation of entry space and transition for guests walking through the passageway through the kitchen to the living room. We selected a rug that ties the exterior colors to the motif and colors of the living. The lemons and leaf pattern on the rug echoes the green and lemons from their garden. Various pieces of pottery in the kitchen share the same colors.

Other Transitional Tricks from Entry to Living Room

Dramatic turmeric-colored drapes framing the living room window draw our eyes forward. When one enters the front door it is important to create eye movement, broadening one's sight line and seeing each layer of depth from one room to the other. Without a glimpse of other rooms, it is easy to feel boxed in or stuck in one space. When our eyes see a succession or glimpses of other rooms our interest is alerted and we gain a sense of directionality. An Ikat-patterned pillow with a brighter shade of yellow gives a splash of color and ties into the turmeric bamboo sheer drapes.

Use of color and texture in materials and furnishings help the eyes explore back and forth and then look to the living room. We coordinated the kitchen and living room colors so that they complemented each other and repeat in each space. The gray/black/white granite countertop color is repeated in a deeper shade of fabric on the sofa. A knitted shawl of nubby, textured black, white and gray mohair wool drapes down a black leather chaise lounge, drawing the eyes down the slope of the chair. The linear kitchen counter of charcoal/black/white granite allows the eye to scan it and then look back at the living room.

We can view wine glasses hanging from a delicate black iron rack located on a wall between the kitchen and living room from the table and bar area. We also view this satisfying composition when leaving the condo.

A butcher block with adjustable fold-down sides is placed at a right angle to the dishwasher. It delineates the kitchen area. This adjustable equipment provides additional prep space and storage for pans and cooking tools. When needed, the sides can be folded down to provide more space for dining.

Rose's swivel-top table is placed parallel to the countertop against the kitchen window. The window overlooks the open area where she is able to view the comings and goings of her neighbors each day. She uses a variety of cloth table mats to add interesting colors and textures.

The living room window acts as a focal point with the combination of dramatic-colored sheers and light streaming in on silvery Guilford Green walls. Dark Mammoth Marmoleum flooring, from the entry to the living room, helps create a grounded, continuous feeling between spaces. We further created emphasis and interest in the living room by including a tweedy charcoal black sofa and multicolored accessories.

Rose's entry plan demonstrates how we organized our thoughts for solutions for her condo. Like doing a jigsaw puzzle we organized a program, space planning, elements and principles of design and details and put them all together while dancing back and forth with different ideas to achieve final design options.

Rose and Larry's future plans include installation of a colourful, dramatic wall. Rose envisions a rich grey wall as a backdrop for a collage of pictures and shelving that will reflect their love for poetry and art.

CASE STUDY 7: A COMPARISON STUDY OF TWO SIMILAR CONDOMINIUM UNITS AT PHOENIX COMMONS, HOMEOWNERS, JYOTI RAE AND ROSE K. MARK, OAKLAND, CALIFORNIA, USA, 2016

This case study illustrates how the interiors of two similar condominium units were designed to reflect differing aesthetics and needs of the occupants. The 624 square feet (57.97 square meters) units each have one bedroom, one bathroom, a shared kitchen/dining room and a living room. Both are end units with wide private outdoor walkways.

Unit 301, Jyoti's unit, situated on the third floor, has a walkway that is partially shaded by the fourth-floor walkway. Rose's walkway in Unit 401 does not have a roof and is exposed to full sun, wind and elements.

The units differ only by the placement of a bedroom closet. Unit 301 has one closet in the bedroom while 401 has an additional closet which decreases the floor space in that room. All other rooms are identical.

Figure 7.4. Simple functional needs are combined with eclectic aesthetic needs.

Source: K. Turcznski.

Jyoti and Rose's lifestyles and functional, aesthetic and emotional needs differ. They designed their interiors to express their individuality.

Interview: Homeowner Jyoti Rae, Unit 301

Rose and your units are almost identical but your homes look very different. What was important to you in designing your small dwelling?

I designed my interior without any assistance or guidance from professionals. I am single, work outside of the home as a social worker and do not entertain much. I wanted my home to reflect the story of my life. Travel, family, nature and color are major themes. My functional needs are simple while my aesthetic needs are widely demonstrated throughout my home.

I love color. Each room in my home is painted with a different color. Adjacent rooms are tied to the other using splashes of colors taken from walls or artwork that can be seen from one room to the other. I surround myself with a rainbow of colors in paintings and displays of my jewelry and scarf collection in my bedroom.

Figure 7.5. Themes and things of importance to the client are used to personalize their interior.

Source: K. Turcznski.

Figure 7.6. Objects from nature bring love of the outdoors to the interior.

Source: K. Turcznski.

When I look around your spaces I see nature, family, color and travel.

Yes, all of those things are important to me. As you can see, on one living room wall I have a collage of artwork from around the world, gathered during 14 years as a Pan American stewardess. My love of travel, encounters with diverse cultures and people I have met are told with each piece of art.

My bathroom, filled with bird nests, plants and a wood dresser with sculpted leaves is my homage to nature. Sculptures, vases and baskets made from clay, plants and wood continue the motif within this room.

Creating floral arrangements is a passionate expression of my appreciation of flowers. I need lots of storage space to hold my collection of over 100 vases. A number of the dressers in my

home are family heirlooms. They hold many of my vases as well as many memories of my family. My collection of vintage travel trunks holds other collections of shoes and art. They double as tables and platforms for my other treasures.

Being in nature is very important to me. I am an avid gardener and the abundance of flowers, vegetables and herbs lining my walkway provides me with a verdant mini garden just a step outside of my unit. Tucked within this setting are two chairs and a table where I can sit, work and watch hummingbirds at my three feeders.

Figure 7.7. A lush deck garden invites peaceful bird watching.

Source: K. Turcznski.

Interview: Homeowner Rose Mark, Unit 401

How do your needs differ from Jyoti's?

Larry and I are both writers and work out of our home. A shared love of poetry, literature, music, food and family unite us in expressing

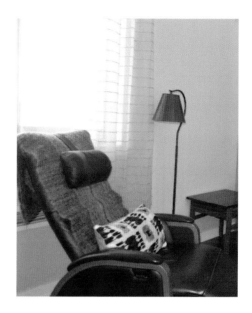

Figure 7.8. A sense of spaciousness is achieved by using placement of furnishings near windows.

Source: K. Turcznski.

our life together. Two workspace areas, an efficient kitchen for everyday cooking and entertaining and a quiet space for reading and listening to music are central for our needs. I require an environment that feels open. Because we work at home, it is extremely important that our workspace is adjustable and does not take over the décor of our home.

Compared to Jyoti's home, what is your function and aesthetic?

Full use is made of every room in our home including our outdoor walkway.

The majority of our furniture is multifunctional in order to utilize every conceivable space and still achieve a sense of openness within our small rooms. Tables have leaves that either fold down or slide closed when used for desks. When we entertain more than two guests these same tables expand to accommodate additional

Figure 7.9. An adaptable space can be used for gardening and entertaining.

Source: K. Turcznski.

diners. They are mid weight and can be easily transported for out-door use. Our butcher block has a drawer and two shelves for storage of large pans, knives, baking sheets, racks and cutting boards. Sides can be flipped down or expanded as needed. Rollers allow easy movement when needed. When more space is needed in the kitchen it can be moved to a different area to serve another purpose.

We use our walkway as a garden and an extended dining room. We have culinary herbs, a dwarf Meyer lemon tree and seasonal vegetables right outside our door. Lemon blossoms perfume the air while red trumpet flowers attract hummingbirds to our feeder. We use a café table with two chairs for intimate dining and with the use of two expandable tables we're able to seat 16 for dinner parties.

Figure 7.10. Elfa shelving for pantry goods and kitchen equipment provides easy access.

Source: K. Turcznski.

The kitchen, our most important room, needs to be efficiently functional as well as welcoming. As shelf space is limited I chose to have sets of six for everyday dishes and bowls. I use the downstairs communal laundry room to free up the kitchen closet for my pantry. Two elfa shelf units with drawers hold silverware, linens, spices, storage containers and miscellaneous cooking equipment.

Three additional shelves were built to hold foodstuffs and cooking equipment that are not used on a daily basis. An elfa shelving system that hangs from the interior door of the pantry closet holds cooking oils, condiments and spices that are used weekly. Pots and pans hang on the remaining wall space on the sides of the shelves. Serving trays are stored in a narrow space under the units.

Our living room window offers a romantic view of neighboring rooftops with a bridge in the background. Sheer turmeric yellow curtains frame and draw attention to look beyond the kitchen to see this aerial tableau. The worktable and entertainment center are lined up and kept close to the wall in order to provide a clear pathway for eyes to journey from the entryway to beyond this window. This contributes to a feeling of airiness in this room.

Figure 7.11. An aerial view of neighboring rooftops gives a feeling of openness in a small living room.

Source: K. Turcznski.

Figure 7.12. A love of music, poetry, and literature is reflected in this cozy living room.

Source: K. Turcznski.

What other functional furnishings do you have?

In the living room, milk crate baskets line the floor under the entertainment shelf unit. Work files fit neatly and conveniently in these containers. They are easily pulled out and pushed back under the shelving as needed. Our TV is hung on the wall to allow shelf room for our extensive CD collection of music from around the world. A custom-built bookshelf with space for more CDs is tucked under the kitchen island in the living room. The island separates and defines each room. Privacy in the living room is achieved with a sofa and chairs that are lower than the height of the island.

The area under the bathroom sink in all the units in this building had a panel of wood covering the pipes. This aesthetic design wasted valuable storage space. With practicality and sustainability in mind, I shared my thoughts with my neighbors. They agreed and took the panels down. I used their discarded panels and had additional shelving made for my bathroom.

Our bedroom space is very limited due to the additional closet. A freestanding shelf sits next to each side of our bed to hold CPAP machines. This allows accessible space needed for pull-out shelves from under the bed. Additional shelves were built in the closets to hold linens and seasonal clothes. A bench is situated across the foot of the bed with milk crate baskets for my work files. This bench is also used for additional seating when needed.

My husband and I have a busy life full of work, entertainment and community activities. Organizing places for important papers and keeping track of mutual schedules helps reduce stress. Entering the unit, a whiteboard calendar is situated out of direct view in the entryway behind the open front door. This helps keep track of our busy work and play schedules. Two white pocket containers under the calendar hold mail or materials for the week. Two additional pocket containers, one for each of us, are situated, out of sight, on the backside of the bedroom door.

The use of multifunctional furnishing and space helps us live in our small dwelling with ease and efficiency.

REFERENCES

Higgins, Ian. 2015. *Spatial Strategies for Interior Design.* London: Laurence King Publishing Ltd. 7.

## CHAPTER 8

TAPPING NATURE AND SUSTAINABILITY FOR SOLUTIONS

Figure 8.1. Hyalite Canyon, Montana. How can you include nature in your design?

Source: S. Halbe.

NATURE, BIOPHILIA AND WELL-BEING

In our previous discussions we learned that our environments affect us. Humans react to the world, whether it is color, the weather or exposure to nature. Many studies indicate positive effects associated with nature, such as presented in *Drunk Tank Pink: And Other Unexpected Forces That Shape How We Think, Feel and Behave* by Adam Alter (2013).

In his seminal book, *Biophilia*, Edward O. Wilson wrote about the relationship between humans and other living systems in nature. He defined biophilia as "the urge to affiliate with other forms of life" (Kellert and Wilson 1993). Since that time there have been numerous studies that indicate that exposure to nature and natural things contribute to human wellness (Schuler, 2016). Biophilic design has evolved from this concept and has been used in designing healthcare and workplace environments. It is also important to include nature in small dwelling design.

Like other aspects of design, biophilic design can be particular to a region or individual tastes. It is important to find out what is important to individual clients during the programming phase. In Chapter 3, *Small Dwelling Programming for Clients*, we provided the exercise *Building in Context*. This survey helps uncover how clients feel about physical exterior elements, natural settings and accessibility to the outdoors. Designers need to investigate physical features in the project, such as sun and climate orientation. What side of the house gets the morning sun? What's the weather like? Is there a view? How important to the client are light, colors and other natural characteristics?

Equally significant is the importance of being connected to other humans. Rosalyn Cama advocates the need for human interaction, another biophilic aspect (Schuler, 2016). In a small dwelling, a view of everyday neighborhood activity might be important to some clients.

Biophilic solutions are not without challenges. Some products that imitate nature are not always sustainable. There are also code compliances and questions about practical health and safety issues with the use of soil, water and other natural features. With all design issues, one needs to weigh all considerations.

Schuler (2016, 50) has addressed the continued development of sustainability with inclusion of biophilic considerations in interior design. When William D. Browning, founding member of the US Green Building Council's board of directors, was asked what word or phrase would acknowledge both human and environmental health, Browning replied "Let's call it good design." We advocate that stance in this book.

INSPIRATION FROM NATURE

We can tune into our environments and find inspiration and ideas from nature. Concepts can be as simple as a natural color scheme and a well-placed window view or as grand as water features and layered lighting. We can produce harmony and unity in our designs similarly to what we find outside. In a small house it is advantageous to relate to the outdoors for the feeling of spaciousness, airiness and, in general, a feeling of well-being. It is helpful to understand the forces that determine how we feel.

This chapter attempts to encourage you to get out into nature. The process of gathering ideas, particularly for an interior design pro-ject, involves taking a break, going outdoors and getting inspired. As discussed in Chapter 6, *Adventures and Exercises in Learning to See Colors* starts with taking a walk or sitting in the park and trying to do nothing but observe and enjoy the day. Take notes, sketch or take photos. How do these environments make you feel? Are you relaxed, comfortable, energized or moved? How could you apply what you see and feel to small dwelling design?

We can learn from nature. Follow the suggestions in the biomimicry exercise in Chapter 5, *Elements and Principles of Design for Small Dwellings*, to get your creative juices flowing. The following example is an exercise that Sherrill gives her Interior Design students. Each time she assigns this biomimicry lesson she is moved and taken back by the thoughtfulness and ingenuity of responses. She is impressed with their keen observations and their care of the earth. She is also impressed by the ideas that they come up with for their designs.

Example of Interior Design Students' Responses

The students are asked to go outside and observe elements of nature that attract them, from the grandest vista to the smallest stone. Here are some of the students' responses.

I could design with diffused and indirect lighting, mimicking the effects of the sun

I would use natural wood or texturing techniques that I took from the growth patterns and textures of tree bark

I would use changes in the height and shape of ceilings to capture changing feelings in space as in forests with different tree canopies

I like interior water features inspired by natural water sounds and visuals, which create relaxation and comfort

What will you discover when you enjoy your day in nature?

Figure 8.2. Diffused and indirect lighting mimics the effects of the sun.

Source: S. Halbe.

WAYS TO INCORPORATE NATURE INTO SMALL DWELLINGS

In a small house residents can profit from the restorative attributes of nature. Get out, get inspired and design your home to feel the rewards. Miller and Schlitt (1985), in *Interior Space: Design Concepts for Personal Needs*, provide a partial list of techniques for designing for naturalness in interiors. Sherrill discusses some of the methods that she has used in her tiny home designs.

> Use light from windows or artificial lighting with coloration that is close to sunlight. Place furniture near natural light. For example, a chair placed near a window

in a sunny, warm spot is rejuvenating. Sun, shining on tile flooring, creates a heat sink and accentuates the warmth. A sky view can be achieved with skylight windows. I have one in my tiny 5 × 7 square feet (1.52 × 2.3 meters)

Figure 8.3. Inspiration can be found in forest ceiling heights and tree root patterns.

Source: S. Halbe.

Figure 8.4. Get out in
nature and get inspired.

Source: S. Halbe.

bathroom and I love to glance up at the trees above or
the moon at night.

Natural materials can be used in so many ways. Wood,
for example, is always wonderful for flooring, but its
texture can be just as exciting as the bark on a tree when
placed on walls, columns or ceilings.

Natural colors: some designers take hikes in nature,
such as the desert, to collect rocks and soil for
inspiration for color schemes. By simply looking out
your window you can come up with the most wonderful
array of silvery greens and grays with the darkness
of brownish black and a hint of blue. Throw in a little

Figure 8.5. A sunny, warm spot is rejuvenating. Sun, shining on tile flooring, creates a heat sink and accentuates the warmth.

Source: Sherrill Baldwin Halbe Interior Design, L. Barber.

contrast of magenta and you have a wonderful color scheme.

Water and plants are always welcomed in the tiniest spaces. I have a waterfall faucet in my bathroom

Figure 8.6. Wood is always wonderful for flooring but can be just as warm and exciting on a wall.

Source: Michael Hospelt Photography, WEISBACH architecture | design, Gar Rector and Associates.

shower/tub. I love it for quick fresh-ups as do my twin granddaughters when they spend the night. Another way to see natural things is to have a view of a well-placed garden or flower box outside.

Nonvisual experiences include the other senses such as natural sound, touch and scents. A fragrant planting as well as a leaf that is soft to the touch can give you hints of soothing nature. The sound of water or birds, even if they are outside, connect us. Always have operable windows so that you can hear and feel the breeze and other natural sights and sounds.

Seasonal changes are usually a welcomed occurrence. Whether or not you can experience the leaves falling in autumn or the snow in the winter you can lay out simple accessories that can help you associate the change.

I enjoy an artist's gourd with natural leaves in the fall. Another easy fix for me, in December, is to take a twiglet of evergreen and place it in a Mason jar with a sprinkle of wax flakes. A sprig of dried or fresh flowers works well in the jar with each new season.

Adding to this list, there are many examples of materials, furnishings and accessories that mimic natural things by their very design – abstract tiles that seem to look like

Figure 8.7. Collected rocks and soil often inspire color schemes.

Source: S. Halbe.

Figure 8.8. Water and plants are always welcomed in the tiniest spaces.

Source: S. Gannon, Gar Rector and Associates, Sherrill Baldwin Halbe Interior Design.

the swirl of sea shells; paintings of natural things – both representative and abstract; tables with twig-like legs. If you are attracted to these looks, perhaps it is because you associate them with nature.

In addition, circadian supportive design can be achieved with attention to window placement and sun orientation. In my living area, I enjoy 270 degrees of changing daylight as the sun shifts, creating different depths of color on each wall and ceiling plane. The height of the windows and eye-level relationships to the sun were major design considerations.

Figure 8.9. This tall, open entrance to the bath and tiny shower accommodates limited space.

Source: S. Gannon, Gar Rector and Associates, Sherrill Baldwin Halbe Interior Design.

Figure 8.10. Terri McKenna's gourd art is displayed in the fall.

Source: T. McKenna, L. Barber.

Figure 8.11. Use furnishings and accessories that mimic nature, such as abstract plants repeated in this rug and painting.

Source: Gar Rector and Associates, S. Halbe.

In the article "Natural Remedy: Biophilic Design Supports Behavioral Health," Clark and Brennan (2017) present four ways to integrate circadian lighting strategies. The first way is explained as,

> **... daylight is the gold standard and is full spectrum, high intensity, and highly variable. Circadian supportive designs should default to daylighting solutions when able and use electric lighting as a supplement. Mimicking daylight patterns and timing should be done in all but the most northern and southern latitudes, where the hours of daylight are reduced and extended light exposure is beneficial. For typical schedules, warm low-intensity light should begin and end the day, with the coolest and brightest intensity occurring midday.**

Attention to spatial planes, such as a staggered corridor, can satisfy curiosity and a meandering feel that is reminiscent in nature. In my cottage, I incorporated vaulted ceilings, rounded wall corners, curved cabinetry and wing walls, which allow the eye to endlessly explore the interior space without feeling uncomfortably enclosed. Nature provides similar movement and layering characteristics.

PRACTICING SUSTAINABILITY AND RESPONSIBILITY

Responsibility for a healthy Earth is growing in awareness and value. As designers, it is our responsibility to always provide knowledge and services related to sustainable practices and materials. The concept of living in a small, efficient dwelling is, in itself, a worthy pursuit.

There are many philosophical ideas and approaches to designing for sustainability. Tucker (2015, 2) advocates an integrated project delivery, "An integrated approach to project delivery involves all team members from the beginning of a project and helps members to make sure they have agreed-upon goals for the sustainability outcomes of the project …"

We believe that the client is also a member of the design team and an important part of the discourse. The designer can interview the client to survey their knowledge and value of sustainability tenets and then review and educate if needed.

As the United States is catching up to Europe, the leader of building sustainability, green products and practices are becoming more and more affordable. Hobbs (2017) notes that many eco-friendly products may be more durable and long-lasting, saving the client money in the long run. It behooves the designer to be aware of cost analyses and to be able to communicate a clear projection of costs and benefits related to sustainable alternatives and methods.

In Case Studies 8 and 9 we present sustainable goals and approaches that Sherrill practiced in designing her own home. Whether it be sourcing locally, using sustainable materials or considering energy efficiency, determine your sustainable goals early on in the project. Utilize *LEED for Homes Simplified Project Checklist*, easily attainable at www.usgbc.com. You will find a descriptive breakdown of the following sustainable goals that you and your client can use in designing their small dwelling:

- **Location and linkages**
- **Innovation and design process**
- **Sustainable sites**
- **Water efficiency**
- **Energy and atmosphere**
- **Materials and resources**
- **Indoor environmental quality**
- **Awareness and education**

CASE STUDY 8: WHERE AND HOW TO IMPLEMENT SUSTAINABILITY PRINCIPLES – A SUSTAINABLE BATHROOM, SHERRILL BALDWIN HALBE INTERIOR DESIGN, BOZEMAN, MONTANA, USA, 2008

Sherrill was put to the challenge of remodeling her own small bathroom using sustainable design knowledge. It was an opportunity to test the principles of sustainable design to the limits and evaluate the process for her clients. She commissioned a contractor who was interested in finding economical and practical ways to incorporate his building skills into the program.

The 60 square feet (5.57 square meters) bathroom was built in the 1980s with typical dark-stained cabinets and a sand-colored sink, toilet and bathtub. The bathroom had little storage and "landings" to place bathroom accessories. Sherrill wanted a functional bathroom, but one that was aesthetically peaceful – a little gem.

Located on the second floor, the window let in the morning sun and provided a vast view of mountains and fields. Sherrill was attentive to the beauty of the view and the importance of preserving nature. Maintaining a small bathroom in itself was an act of sustainability and drove the designer's concept.

What were your immediate goals in designing your bathroom?

With the belief that "green design is just good design," I was able to create an efficient, safe, healthy and aesthetic space with the guidance of six Rs of sustainable design: research, reduction, reuse, reclaim, recycle–salvage, and recycle. Sustainable design should be integral to interior design. When I remodeled my master bathroom, I wanted to put my personal actions "where my mouth was."

My first goal was to use as much of the existing bathroom as possible (and not contribute to the landfill) and the second was to design with local workers, artisans and materials in mind. The first R, research, was extensive, but now it is part of my repertoire of knowledge for future projects.

Figure 8.12. Decorative wrought iron stands are used for hanging towels and holding accessories.

Source: Sherrill Baldwin Halbe Interior Design, L. Barber.

How did you address the other Rs to make the design sustainable?

I used the existing footprint of the bathroom and included unusual fixtures for storage such as a blanket rack for hanging towels and a decorative wrought iron stand for folded towels and accessories. They are airy and whimsical but work functionally.

The original sink and bathtub were in good shape, although dated in color. I decided to keep them and select a tile treatment that

Figure 8.13. The recycled counter top travertine tiles were honed for a contemporary look.

Source: Sherrill Baldwin Halbe Interior Design, L. Barber.

Figure 8.14. The existing cabinet was faux painted by a local artisan. Another artisan made the mirrors out of old picture frames and a window.

Source: Sherrill Baldwin Halbe Interior Design, L. Barber.

Figure 8.15. A reused natural, muslin shower curtain and mirrors allude to spatial width.

Source: Sherrill Baldwin Halbe Interior Design, L. Barber.

aesthetically melded the color of the sink, bathtub and toilet to the updated tile.

I reused the existing oak sink cabinet and had it faux painted by a local artisan. The cabinets took on a patina of complementary colors. Another artisan took old window and picture frames and made them into mirrors.

I maintained the ambient fluorescent lighting, but added an antique fixture for task and accent lighting.

I reused a natural, muslin shower curtain and tucked it behind a used green cotton drape, which, with mirrors, spatially alluded to width. I used cotton rugs and linens as other natural products.

Figure 8.16. Ambient fluorescent lighting was retained with the addition of an antique fixture for task and accent.

Source: Sherrill Baldwin Halbe Interior Design, L. Barber.

Did you buy any new or reused materials or accessories?

I selected used travertine tiles for the sink counter. I didn't like the outdated sheen so I had a local tile contractor hone them down for a more contemporary look.

Figure 8.17. The tile treatment melds with existing sand color of the sink and tub.

Source: Sherrill Baldwin Halbe Interior Design, L. Barber.

I discovered some old store fixtures in a local shop and reused them as towel and drapery holders.

Custom-colored, no-VOC paint was purchased from a local store that specialized in sustainable products.

What other recycled materials did you use?

I used a window shade that was made of recycled paper, which provided privacy and filtered natural light.

For a pattern accent around the bathtub and sink area, I selected recycled glass tile made by a local artisan.

You mentioned that the contractor was local. What other measures did you use to take advantage of local services and materials?

The contractor lived in the neighborhood and was willing to help me obtain my sustainable goals. He literally had a two-minute commute, which he liked. He was enthusiastic about the sustainable challenge and was very creative in reusing cabinets, old lumber and materials.

Other crafts persons were also local, which cut down on their commute time and transportation costs.

Figure 8.18. Towel and drapery holders were reused store fixtures from a local shop.

Source: Sherrill Baldwin Halbe Interior Design, L. Barber.

Figure 8.19. Paintings were created by local artists.

Source: Sherrill Baldwin Halbe Interior Design, L. Barber.

We donated all useable, discarded materials to local agencies such as Habitat for Humanity or stored them for other projects.

I hung local artists' paintings on the wall.

When we read Part 1, we learned about how to identify the clients' needs when planning a small home. Then in Part 2 we looked at how design theory, space planning, design development and attention to human considerations contribute to the design process of fulfilling these needs. Residential interior design, after all, is planning many parts and putting them together for the health, safety and well-being of the client.

Part 3 of this book addresses some major small dwelling issues and how to solve these specific design problems. We provide design tips to ease your client's questions about where to store things; how to make a small kitchen work efficiently; ideas on furnishings and accessories that take up less room; ways to stay within the budget; and how to entertain with limited space. *Practical Solutions for Living Well in a Small Dwelling* comes to your rescue with innovative and light-hearted ideas for successfully implementing your clients' important requirements.

REFERENCES

Alter, Adam. 2013. *Drunk Tank Pink: And Other Unexpected Forces That Shape How We Think, Feel and Behave.* New York, NY: Penguin Services.

Clark, Ed and Marty Brennan, eds. 2017. "Natural Remedy: Biophilic Design Supports Behavioral Health." *Healthcare Design.* Accessed August 3, 2017. www.healthcaredesignmagazine.com/projects/ natural-remedy-biophilic-design-supports-behavioral.

Hobbs, Cathy. 2017. Tribune News Service. www.detroitnews.com/story/ life/home-garden/2017/01/19/create-sustainable-energy-efficient-home/ 96793596. Accessed January 20, 2017.

LEED for Homes Simplified Project Checklist. www.usgbc.com. Accessed April 4, 2017.

Kellert, Stephen R. and Edward O. Wilson. 1993. *Biophilia.* Washington, DC: Island Press. 416.

Miller, Stuart and Judith K. Schlitt. 1985. *Interior Space: Design Concepts for Personal Needs.* New York, NY: Praeger.

Schuler, Timothy A. 2016. "Let Nature In." *ASID ICON.* Washington, DC.

Tucker, Lisa M. 2015. *Designing Sustainable Residential and Commercial Interiors: Applying Concepts and Practices.* New York, NY: Fairchild Books. 2.

## Part 3

PRACTICAL SOLUTIONS FOR LIVING WELL IN A SMALL DWELLING

Chapters 9–13

CHAPTER 9

FINDING STORAGE SPACE

NONLINEAR APPROACHES

Storage space is at a premium in small dwellings. Often our view of available spaces is limited to counter tops, shelves, drawers and cupboards. Let's take a nonlinear approach to viewing space by looking above, under, behind and in between. Unused spaces can be found on ceilings, walls and adjacent spaces between walls and large appliances. The insides of cabinet doors and undersides of shelves are seldom used. Negative spaces between objects are unused spaces waiting to be utilized. Let's take a look at ceiling and wall space solutions and then consider typical storage problems and solutions in other areas. Rose features the following ideas for clients, which can be very useful information for the designer when design small dwellings.

Figure 9.1. Placement of shelves near the ceiling allows more open space closer to seating area.

Source: C. Barry.

Ceilings

Typical rooms in the United States are 8–9 feet (2.44–2.74 meters) in height. Older buildings can range upwards to 14 feet (4.27 meters) or more. With this in mind, think of all the space above you that's available for use. Imagine all the things you could have within easy reach.

Figure 9.2. Tall cabinets were built for a very tall person.

Source: C. Barry.

My friend Jorge is very tall and extremely creative. He installed two kitchen cabinets starting from the ceiling. He staggered the depth of each one with the top cabinet deeper than the one under it. This accomplished two purposes. It was aesthetically pleasing as well as functional. Keeping the same shape, design, color, width and height of these units created a compactness that continued an overall modernist design theme. Having the depth of the top cabinet deeper than the lower cabinet added an element of movement. Jorge placed a flat glass menu board under the small cabinet to complete the succession of size and movement. He stored large, infrequently used platters and equipment in these cabinets. Form and functionality were employed beautifully here.

Ceiling racks are the most obvious solution. They come in a variety of sizes, shapes, weights and configurations. Most commonly used for hanging pots and pans, they can also hold cooking tools as well. Make sure you store your heavy pots and pans on a shelf that is mid-level for both safety and ergonomic purposes. Hang only those that you use weekly or monthly. Hang them near prep areas or within

Figure 9.3. Every surface on a circular pot rack is used.

Source: C. Barry.

191

Figure 9.4. An out-of-the-way place was found for a speaker in the kitchen.

Source: C. Barry.

reach of the stove. Store the rest on lower shelves in the kitchen or an auxiliary room.

Circular ceiling racks holding colorful or metal cooking tools have the potential for delighting the eyes and maybe the ears, depending upon the use of color and sounds of metal clinking against each other.

My friend Dan made a little ledge close to the ceiling in his kitchen to house a small speaker. Out of the way, it is located in an area that provides music for kitchen, deck and dining room.

Walls and Adjacent Spaces between Walls and Large Appliances

Wall space is typically used from the waist up to arm's reach. What about the space below the waist? What about the space that is above hand reach?

Two or three tiered shelves can provide additional storage space with less used items on the highest rung. Baking racks can be hung above with S hooks affixed to the grids for hanging measuring cups, spoons and other baking tools. Having all these tools in the same place makes baking much easier and efficient.

If space allows, narrow shelves, perhaps no deeper than five inches, can be built below the waist area against a wall. Due to the close proximity to the floor, make sure items kept on these shelves are covered.

Figure 9.5. Multipurpose racks take up less space on tiny counters.

Source: Sherrill Baldwin Halbe Interior Design, S. Gannon.

Wall racks and grids are also commonly used when there is space available on walls. Single-line racks can be extended or arranged in configurations to fit limited space. Arranging them in staggered lines can create interesting, aesthetically pleasing designs.

Areas between refrigerator, stoves and established walls are handy to slide folding furnishings such as TV tray tables or a step stool. Many older homes have shallow cabinet space that once held fold-down ironing boards. These spots can hold narrow shelves of spices or less bulky items.

Any kind of rack can be charming and useful.

SOLUTIONS TO COMMON PROBLEMS

I don't have enough counter space or shelves to hold my supplies.

Rolling shelves with butcher block counters are the most popular solution used to provide additional counter and storage space. You can find them in a myriad of sizes and price ranges. Some have countertops that can be used for prepping as well as for eating. Others have multiple shelves for storage. Wired basket shelving allows an open view of contents. Inexpensive and lightweight wire or plastic rolling storage units can be found at office or school supply stores. Many of these carts have seven to eight drawers where lightweight cooking supplies, such as spices and foodstuffs, can be kept.

Some fixed shelving can be arranged with enough space between each to utilize the top and underside. Hooks can be attached to the underside for hanging cups and mugs. Decorative brackets with hooks can serve a dual purpose for supporting shelves as well as for hanging items.

The counter space next to my kitchen sink is so small. I don't have enough room for a dish drainer rack.

Figure 9.6. An example of using above, below, and side surfaces.

Source: C. Barry.

Use the dishwasher to hold clean dishes or do it the old-fashioned way and lay down a dishtowel for your dishes and pots to drain. Microfiber draining cloths are easy to wring or launder and dry out.

If you are in the market for a dishwasher, consider the dual washer style with two drawer units stacked in one appliance. You can keep track of clean dishes in one drawer and dirty dishes in another.

I don't have enough drawer space much less room in them for eating utensils.

Conventional silverware or flatware trays often do not use up the entire space in a drawer. Measure the width, depth and length of unused space and pick up narrow trays to fill in the extra space.

Inexpensive classroom pencil trays can be found at teacher or office supply stores. Chopsticks, extra sets of dinnerware or cheese knives fit handily into these narrow containers. Line up sets of eating utensils in opposing directions to use up the negative space where the handles lie.

Figure 9.7. Pots and pans line a rack for easy storage and accessibility.

Source: C. Barry.

Partitioned upright containers for holding silverware take up very little space on counters and tables. Styles range from casual basquetry to modern glass.

I can't fit my baking cookie pans and racks anywhere. They're just too tall and wide for my cupboards.

That space under the sink is not just for garbage and cleaning supplies. Flat items such as baking sheets and racks can be stored there. Use the rack from your roaster to keep them upright, as pictured in Chapter 11, *Choosing Furnishings and Accessories that*

Figure 9.8. Partitioned upright containers for holding silverware take up very little space on counters.

Source: S. Halbe.

are *Multifunctional, Flexible and Adjustable*. You can also purchase storage racks. Make room by putting cleaning supplies in a caddy or bucket for easy transport. Keep surplus supplies in a closet or, better yet, buy only enough for current use.

I don't have enough drawers for my kitchen tools and the few I have are so deep I can't find anything in them.

Measure the depth, width and length of each drawer. Categorize utensils that go together and purchase separate washable containers to house each category of tools

Figure 9.9. A variety of arrangements adds interest to the eye.

Source: C. Barry.

Store kitchen tools upright in containers for saving space and easier viewing.

I don't have enough room in my cupboard to fit all my plates, bowls, serving pieces and cooking tools.

Place individual lightweight serving plates flat against the back wall of a cupboard to frame nesting stacks of plates, bowls and glassware. Use stick-on hooks to hold lightweight items, such as strainers, measuring cups, cooking tools on the inside of the cupboard door.

I have a tiny bathroom with limited storage shelves.

Clutter makes a room look smaller. It's important to prioritize the things you use daily and weekly and put them in containers or baskets near areas where you'll be using them.

If there is space under the sink, counters or near the toilet area, utilize these spaces to hold things you would normally use such as rolls of toilet paper, soaps, lotions and hair products. Put them in interesting containers without covers to create compositions of shapes, textures and color. Store things like hair dryers and appliances out of sight.

Setting up shelves using simple brackets with wood or glass platforms is fairly easy and inexpensive. Glass shelves can lighten a small and narrow room. Staggering shelves can break up space and provide a feeling of spaciousness. If using a series of shelves to hold items, play around with the size and shapes you create when you arrange your things. Large or heavier items on the bottom will ground your room while the ascending smaller items will draw eyes upward. Heavier items on the top with lighter smaller items on the bottom will give the illusion of being weighted down; probably not a good idea nor a good feeling in a small room unless the heavier items are broken up with intermediate-sized objects.

Figure 9.10. Glass shelving lightens and opens up room.

Source: C. Barry.

I have limited space for a dining room table and I enjoy having dinner parties with six or more guests. How can I accomplish this in a small area?

Figure 9.11. Translucent bedroom closet doors provide a creative storage solution.

Source: Michael Hospelt Photography, WEISBACH architecture | design, Gar Rector and Associates.

Drop-leaf and gate-leg tables are so adaptable for small areas. When sides are folded down they take up less space. When sides are flipped up and leaves inserted they extend to seat more guests. Some have drawers for additional storage. Rounded ends can allow more seating. They can become small enough for seating two to four and others extend to accommodate 12 people.

I really love my collection of boots, shoes and hats. I really need somewhere to store them where they are visible and I can readily select them for the day. I need closet ideas.

Figure 9.12. A tiny room near the bedroom works well as a walk-in closet.

Source: S. and G. Rector, S. Halbe.

Learn to look beyond ordinary solutions and use different spaces creatively. For example, Christy set up a colorful wall in her bedroom to store numerous shoes and boots. Sarah utilized a tiny room near her bedroom. She had a door built in the bedroom that entered the small space, which became her walk-in closet.

## CHAPTER 10

THE SMALL KITCHEN

Figure 10.1. The custom
refrigerator fits the needs of
a tall client.

Source: C. Barry.

SPACE PLANNING

Space planning for kitchen design requires a thorough look at who
will be cooking the majority of time, how often the kitchen will be
used and specific physical needs. Find out what types of food will be
cooked most often and whether this area will be used for entertaining
or other activities, such as laundry, etc.

Individualizing the needs of your client can make this room a wonderful place for creativity. Built-in bins for flour or staple items, such
as beans or rice for cultures that use these items daily, are good
uses of space. Adjustable or lowered counters can provide accessibility for wheelchairs or individuals of different heights. Choosing
the most efficient stove fan to fit the type of food being prepared
is just as important, especially when high heat or volatile oils are

being used. Seating areas as well as counters can be designed for multipurpose use if the kitchen will be used for entertaining. All the while, one needs to consider the budget, local codes and the client's desire for an open or enclosed kitchen arrangement.

One can save time, energy and money in a small kitchen. This chapter addresses the aforementioned criteria and informs the reader about essential kitchen space planning, appliances and tools for food preparation and culling techniques. This information is valuable for designers to understand so that they can guide their clients' choices.

First of all, you need to know more about your client and their relationship to their kitchen. We have provided exercises with examples and worksheets in Appendix A.

Use the information gained from this *Kitchen Use Questionnaire* to have a discussion with your client about specific needs or features that would be appreciated in their kitchen.

Kitchen Use Questionnaire for your Client

1.   **How many people typically cook in the kitchen?**

My husband and I take turns cooking. Occasionally, we both cook at the same time. On the weekends the kids cook with us.

2.   **How often does someone cook in your kitchen?**

Breakfast

Mostly light breakfasts during the week with more elaborate brunches on weekends

Lunch

Daily lunch

Dinner

Most evenings

3. Do you or anyone in your household need any space, material or height considerations in the kitchen?

My husband is tall and I am short. We both cook.

4. What types of food and/or items do you consider staples in your kitchen?

We eat a lot of rice and use a rice cooker.

5. How often do you entertain guests?

Our three adult children eat dinner with us every Sunday.

6. Do you include your guests in the kitchen or do you entertain them in another room?

Everyone in the family helps out in the kitchen. When we entertain friends, they sit in the living room.

7. Will you use the kitchen space for other activities?

The children usually do their homework at the kitchen table.

8. Would you rather have an open kitchen to the other rooms or a kitchen that is enclosed?

We prefer an open kitchen, but I would like to screen off some of the messy areas. I like a clean kitchen.

ESSENTIAL KITCHEN EQUIPMENT FOR FOOD PREPARATION

Discussion

The kitchen is often the busiest and most active room in the house. Choosing appliances and cooking tools that fit the needs of the client can influence ease or difficulty in preparing a meal. Having just the right tool nearby can affect an individual's efficiency and mood. You, as a designer, can help your client analyze their needs with the following discussions and exercises.

A food processor, stand-up mixer, coffee maker and coffee grinders are some of the more popular kitchen appliances one might find in the kitchen. Ask your client to consider whether they need a hand mixer or stand-up mixer. How much baking do they do? If they're an occasional baker then a hand mixer makes sense. However, if they love to bake, especially bread products, then the stand-up mixer or food processor is for them.

Does one need a full-size, mini or food processor at all? If your client is not interested in cooking, then skip these two. However, if your client enjoys cooking, these appliances are indispensable for shortening preparation time.

Having a tool that works efficiently makes an enormous difference. Cutting through a hot crusty loaf of bread with a dull knife and

Figure 10.2. A built-in, two-drawer energy-efficient dishwasher works well for small families.

Source: Sherrill Baldwin Halbe Interior Design, L. Barber.

seeing that beautiful bread being mangled and crushed can be a disappointing and frustrating experience. It is important to have the right tool for the job. A good serrated bread knife cuts through bread and saves time and effort. It's an investment for creating ease and pleasure in the kitchen. Conversely, appliances that take more time to set up than to function can be annoying.

The basic challenge in a small kitchen is shortage of space. Ask your client if they want to have a dishwasher or more space for storage. Think in terms of needs. A dishwasher might not be the most efficient use of space if there are just one or two family members or they don't entertain. This space may be utilized for a better purpose. However, if your client's household or lifestyle includes lots of entertaining or kids, then a dishwasher might be a necessary energy and time saver.

There are many gadgets on the market that appear to save time but take up storage space. Which ones are used the most? Which ones are used on occasion, like a fondue pot?

Have your client make a list of all their cooking appliances and tools. Have them list their things in groups. What do they use every day, week, month, once a year or once in a blue moon? They can place those items that are used daily or weekly in an accessible place. They can label and place the ones used once a month or for parties in a box on a less reachable shelf. The "once a year" things can be stored where they keep their occasional equipment. They may want to send the rest out to the universe for someone else to enjoy.

Of course, there are those pans, gadgets and tools that hold sentimental memories that one never gives up. Ask your client to find additional uses for them, such as a decorative conversation piece. If they can be used in a functional capacity, that's even better. Rose has three sets of mortar and pestles in varying sizes that she uses once a month. They sit on her counter holding garlic, shallots and dried herbs when not in active use. It's convenient, decorative and serves more than one purpose.

Discuss and help your client take action. For example, you might say,

Now, it's time to figure out where to place the utensils you'll be using. What tools do you use on a daily basis? Place daily cooking implements and equipment within close proximity to prep area. For example, go-to cooking tools can hang on a rack right next to the stove while extra tools can be placed in containers nearby. Situate prep areas as close to the stove and sink as possible. Pots and pans are best placed close by but away from the stove area because they attract oil from cooking and can crowd out workspace.

The good thing about small kitchens is that things are close at hand or within easy reach. If the ceiling is high enough to hold a hanging pot rack, make sure there is adequate space between the stove and rack to allow freedom of movement. One may not have as much control over the amount of space available but look for possibilities using a non-linear approach. Chapter 9, *Finding Storage Space*, can help you find these nontraditional places.

Ask your clients what kitchen equipment they have or plan to acquire. Help them consider appliances that are convenient and ergonomically functional. Use worksheets in Appendix A.

Kitchen Appliances and Tools: How Many Do You Have and How Many Do You Need?

Exercise Example for Client

Please list each kitchen appliance and check how often you use it.

Appliance	Daily	Weekly	Monthly	Yearly	Once in a Blue Moon
Mixer		x			
Platter				x	
Tea cups	x				

HOW MUCH FOOD DO YOU BUY?

Go over the following discussion with your client to identify the storage space that they will need. Ask your client some of the questions that Rose poses. Rose also presents a list of questions about kitchen and eating routines and provides a purchasing exercise with an example.

DISCUSSION

Organization and efficiency are time, energy and money savers. How many times have you looked in your refrigerator or pantry for an item that you just knew you had but couldn't find? Weeks or months later, it magically appears. Had they shifted forward while you searched for other items? What a waste of time and money buying what you already owned. Help your client organize foods by category and encourage your client to store them in the same area.

Ask your client if they buy just enough food for a week or do they tend to stockpile for a rainy day because it was a bargain? How many condiments do they really need to have in the refrigerator? If storage space is limited and they don't have an extra fridge, a bit of mindfulness might save them a lot of time and frustration.

I'm a condiment junkie. I'll admit it. I have about a refrigerator shelf worth of different condiment sauces. I cook a wide range of ethnic dishes and am always researching new cuisines so it's part of my research lab. But still, do I really need a large jar of sun-dried tomatoes or the super jumbo size jar of mayonnaise? Buying food that spoils or becomes stale before you have a chance to use it is not economical.

Much depends upon how often we use these foodstuffs and their shelf life. Everyone has recipes they make on a regular basis. Some people eat salads every day. Buying salad greens in bulk makes sense. Onions, garlic, chicken stock, garbanzo beans and pasta are staples in my house so I buy these in large bags or by the case. I eat less than one pound of potatoes each month. However, I eat rice once or twice a week so buying 25 pounds (11.36 kg) of rice rather than potatoes makes sense for me.

We have provided example exercises to use with your clients and worksheets in Appendix A.

Purchasing Inventory Exercise Example for your Client

Every kitchen is as individual as the people who use it. What is your client's life in the kitchen?

What type of food do you and your family eat weekly?

We eat simple fast breakfasts such as eggs, yoghurt and fruit.

We eat sandwiches or leftovers for lunch.

We love to cook foods from different cultures that concentrate on lots of vegetables and grains with small amounts of meat.

How much meat, poultry, fish, dairy, grains or beans do you eat?

We eat a variety of chicken, fish and some red meat. We have some kind of grains and beans three times or more a week.

What items do you buy each week?

We buy one dozen eggs, a quart of milk, fresh vegetables and fruit.

What ingredients do you typically use each week or month?

We use olive oil, yoghurt, vegetables, fruit and a variety of meats and fish.

How many meals do you cook during the week?

We typically cook three to four times a week.

Which meal do you cook the most?

We cook dinner the most since we often use it for lunch and leftovers.

What types of meals do you cook, such as Italian, Chinese, Latin, Indian or Middle Eastern?

We like to cook food from all over the world but for the last year we've been cooking lots of Middle Eastern food

Purchasing Exercise Example for your Client

Look over what food products your client typically uses. Which items have a good shelf life such as granola, oatmeal, yoghurt, bread, meats, potatoes, pasta and bottled sauces. If they use them every week or every month then these would be the best in bulk. Otherwise, they can buy shorter shelf life items such as milk, eggs and perishable vegetables weekly.

We have provided an example exercise to use with your clients and worksheets in Appendix A that can help you organize and plan your food purchases.

Make a list of each meal you prepare or serve daily. Write down what you serve during the week for each meal. Then write down the ingredients you need to prepare these meals.

Breakfast   Cold cereal, toast, eggs or take out

Lunch   Bring lunch or eat out

Dinner   Fast food, ready-made food or prepared
meals

Typical meal for weekday:

Breakfast Yoghurt, fruit, granola, toast, eggs, bacon, sausage, oatmeal

Lunch Sandwiches, colds cuts, tuna, eggs, salads, leftovers

Dinner Chicken, beef, pork, fish, salad, type of pasta, spaghetti sauces, chili

Typical meal for weekend:

Breakfast Eggs, potatoes, bacon, sausage, pancakes

Lunch Eat out or sandwiches

Dinner Eat out or meals with beef, pork, fish, pasta, etc.

Number of items needed to make weekly meals:

Breakfast 32 ounces (907 grams) yoghurt, 3 pounds (1.30 kilograms) fresh fruit, 1 dozen eggs

Lunch 1 pound (.45 kilogram) cold cuts, 1 pound (.45 kilograms) deli cheese, 1 loaf bread

Dinner 1 pound (.45 kilograms) beef, 1 chicken, 1 pound (.45 kilograms) pork, 3 pounds (1.36 kilograms) greens

CASE STUDY 9: PUTTING DOWN ROOTS: A KITCHEN AND DINING ROOM REMODEL, SHERRILL BALDWIN HALBE INTERIOR DESIGN, BOZEMAN, MONTANA, USA, 2008

Sherrill took on the challenge of designing a kitchen and dining room that would reflect her values and activities in a home that would become a place of putting down roots. It was also an opportunity to test the principles of sustainable design to the limits. Her contractor, who was interested in finding economical and practical ways to incorporate his building skills into the program, agreed to do the job.

The 1980s kitchen and dining room spaces were small, but with a 100 square feet (9.29 square meters) addition, Sherrill was able to include the functionality and aesthetics that she wanted. The

Figure 10.3. Existing oak cabinets were used by scraping off the 1980s dark stain with an inexpensive scraping tool.

Source: Sherrill Baldwin Halbe Interior Design, L. Barber.

site's rural characteristics and woodsy views, in part, determined the space plan and ultimately the design concept.

The design concept was also driven by the creativity of cooking. Sherrill, a former restaurateur, with a grown family steeped in making good food, needed a kitchen and dining room that would accommodate people, equipment and supplies when entertaining big and small events.

Sherrill has woven sustainable methods and materials into this design and has created a kitchen and dining room that reflect the natural landscape of the outside and the beauty of recycled materials of rusts, copper and wood. Fresh food and accoutrements only complement the setting.

What was your process as both designer and client in the programming phase of the design?

In the programming phase, I had an interesting awareness that I wasn't quite sure of how our last home should look. After years of designing for clients and enjoying the mutual involvement of choosing various styles and materials, I was at a loss for what I wanted for this house. In the end I realized that the overwhelming beauty of the outdoors, interest in food and family and the theme of sustainability would influence my decision in colors and finishes.

Concurrently, when analyzing the design concept, I recalled an invitation to an art show that I had recently received. A lusty abstract sculpture constructed of rusted metal, weathered and burnt wood and copper was pictured on the invitation. The found-object sculpture triggered an epiphany and realization that this was the palette that I wanted. It was a metaphor of sustainability and what I prized in my kitchen.

Driven by sustainable goals, how did you solve some of the problems in this older kitchen and dining room?

For this design I used as much of the existing kitchen as possible and teamed up with local workers and artisans. I also used as many local materials as I could find.

I contracted the remodel project with a creative, skillful builder who was willing to research sustainable remodel solutions. He also lived in the neighborhood, which cut down on his transportation.

I expanded the needed dining room space by pushing the kitchen footprint into a small addition, which not only created space, but gave potential access to a deck, morning sun and rural views.

Figure 10.4. The old cabinet doors were livened up by replacing some of the dated glass with reclaimed gravel screen from Big Timberworks, Inc.

Source: Sherrill Baldwin Halbe Interior Design, L. Barber.

Figure 10.5. The designer locally sourced tile for the floors, countertop and backsplash.

Source: Sherrill Baldwin Halbe Interior Design, L. Barber.

The builder used some recycled lumber in building the addition and energy-efficient windows, made with certified wood. We insulated the addition and painted the walls with non-VOC paint. The contractor plumbed radiant heat in the flooring.

The contractor scraped off the 1980s dark stain on the existing oak cabinets using a very effective, inexpensive scraping tool. We rearranged all of the cabinets so that they would function according to my work patterns. We specified certified wood and finished some of the cabinets to match the old wood. We painted other cabinets a neutralized green. I livened up the cabinet doors by replacing some of the dated glass with reclaimed gravel screen from Big Timberworks, Inc., a local company that specialized in creative reuses of materials.

I selected tile, made in the US, for the floors, countertop and backsplash.

The tile flooring, in part, acts as a heat sink for passive solar heating from the new windows and doors.

I used EcoVeil MechoSystems for shading the operable, ventilating windows. The shades are PVC-free and fully recyclable (the shades can be sent back to the factory to be recycled).

I selected a built-in two-drawer, energy-efficient dishwasher and a recycle unit that separates recyclable trash. We also included a compost receptacle.

I reused the existing stove, microwave, re-faced trash compactor and refrigerator. The refrigerator was replaced later.

I maintained the ambient fluorescent fixtures and added efficient under-counter task and accent lighting.

Local artisans made the jelly cabinet, copper mirror, recycled rag rug, artwork and other accessories. I reused my antique buffets, a wool rug, draperies and the family kitchen table and chairs.

We gave all useable, discarded materials to local agencies such as Habitat for Humanity or stored them for other projects.

Figure 10.6. The jelly cabinet, recycled rag rug, artwork and other accessories were made by local artisans.

Source: Sherrill Baldwin Halbe Interior Design, L. Barber.

You had size and structural constraints to deal with in the space planning. How did the space ultimately lend itself to your lifestyle of leading a quiet life with your husband juxtaposed to entertaining big and small crowds?

We opened up the new addition space with great views of outdoor greenery and mountains. We placed a small family table in this area where my husband and I have most of our meals. Cleanup activities and some food preparation are done in this space and we have access to an outdoor deck. We keep tubs of summer and fall plantings on the deck and process our harvest in this sink area. This area is quite intimate.

For larger food preparations we use the whole kitchen and utilize the peninsula for serving. The dining table is close at hand for sit-down parties. We have everything from seafood boils on newspaper to six-course dinners. All supplies and equipment are close at hand.

The living room is relatively smaller than the kitchen and dining room. Was that by design?

Yes, our priority of function and activities in the kitchen and dining room determined the allotment of space. We use the dining room for other functions so the space is frequently used. My office is in the next room and the table makes a good layout area. The living room is smaller and more intimate.

## CHAPTER 11

CHOOSING FURNISHINGS AND ACCESSORIES THAT ARE MULTIFUNCTIONAL, FLEXIBLE AND ADJUSTABLE

HOW MANY DIFFERENT WAYS CAN YOU USE HOUSEHOLD ITEMS?

In small dwellings, space is at a premium. Using furniture and tools that provide more than one function is one solution. Furniture that can be folded, nested or stacked saves space and is easily moved from place to place. You can guide your client with our discussions and start looking for items on the following lists that are collapsible, foldable and adjustable, which can save you space.

1. Baskets for storage that can be placed behind or under benches, tables or shelves

2. Coat and umbrella trees or hooks

3. Folding step stools or chairs that can double for seating or display

4. Tables that fold down or have removable leaves

5. Racks for shoes

Figure 11.1. **This table seats four, six or eight and can adjust to coffee table or dining table height.**

Source: R. Mark.

Figure 11.2. Artwork above coat hooks softens wall space and adds interest to area.

Source: C. Barry.

Figure 11.3. Stools or chairs can double for seating or display.

Source: S. Halbe.

Figure 11.4. Racks are handy for shoes and displays.

Source: S. Halbe.

Figure 11.5. Rack and shelves for the kitchen are functional and decorative.

Source: S. Halbe.

Figure 11.6. Built-in hinged tables that collapse provide adjustability.

Source: S. Gannon.

Figure 11.7. A variety of kitchen tools on rack provides visual interest and easy access for the cook.

Source: C. Barry.

6. Reclining sofas
7. Sofa beds
8. Murphy beds
9. Moveable screens
10. Stairs with storage in steps
11. Adjustable heights on coffee tables and desks
12. Racks and shelves for the kitchen
13. Built-in hinged tables that collapse
14. Lawn and camping furniture
15. Storage in ovens for baking pans or pots

OTHER DOUBLE-DUTY IDEAS THAT CAN BE USED AND WHERE

Here are a few examples of furnishings and tools that can do double duty for your client.

In the Living Room and Dining Room

A long bench can serve as a landing platform for keys and things you need when entering or exiting the house. It can also be relocated and used for seating or as an additional coffee table.

Extra dining room chairs can double as night tables when placed on each side of the bed.

A cedar chest used to store extra blankets or clothes can be used as a coffee table or to provide extra seating when needed.

Attractive tray tables lined up by two or three make an interesting coffee table arrangement or cocktail buffet table. They don't take up much space when used individually in different rooms or when collapsed.

Figure 11.8. A low bookshelf can double as a seating area and hold a television and other accessories.

Source: C. Barry.

Nesting tables come in a variety of sizes, shapes and designs. When not in use they can nest into a compact space.

A low bookshelf can double as a seating area, hold a television or become a place to show off your accessories.

An ottoman can double as a coffee table or hold storage space within.

Adjustable and flexible floor or hanging lamps that can stretch, bend or reach more than one area open up more surface space.

Tables with adjustable legs can be lengthened or shortened for regular dining table or coffee table heights.

Figure 11.9. A hanging rack for clothes in the laundry room can provide additional storage.

Source: C. Barry.

Dining tables with sides that can be folded down can accommodate small spaces.
Dining tables that have leaves are handy for expansion of table space.

Laundry Room

Hanging racks for clothes and extra hangers can double for laundry and extra hanging storage.

Outdoor Furniture

Attractive folding chairs can double for inside and outside use. You can fold and store them outside when not in use.

Sturdy storage tool chests can also double for extra seating as needed.

Figure 11.10. Take the doors off an unused closet and insert the bed for more room.

Source: G. and S Rector, S. Halbe.

In the Bedroom

Take the doors off an unused closet and insert the bed for more room.

Figure 11.11. An additional mirrored medicine cabinet provides more storage and depth to the room.

Source: C. Barry.

Over-door hanging mirrors with storage compartments can house jewelry, etc.

In the Bathroom

Place an out-of-the-way medicine cabinet to mirror a tiny bathroom and add depth.
Use a bathroom door with an opaque window to let in light. Place a towel rack below.

In the Kitchen

Figure 11.12. A kitchen peninsula functions as a work area and a place to eat.

Source: Sherrill Baldwin Halbe Interior Design, L. Barber.

Kitchen stools can be used for seating as well as countertop areas to hold a food processor, stand-up mixer or blender as needed.
Folding step stools can double for seating or a plant holder.

A kitchen peninsula can function as a work area, a place to eat or a platform for bar supplies.

Figure 11.13. A wire baking rack works well for hanging measuring cups and other tools.

Source: C. Barry.

Hang measuring spoons, cups and other baking tools on wire baking racks mounted on the wall. This arrangement saves drawer space as well as giving quick access to tools. Arrange them into a collage of shapes and color as an art statement.

Collapsible butcher board carts with wheels offer compactness and mobility.

The lattice basket within a lettuce spinner can function as a strainer, colander and cheese mold. Pasta, vegetables and fruit drain nicely in it.

Is the rack in the turkey pan in the way? Take it out and use it for a lid holder or for baking sheets and pans. Baskets used for decorative use can double as food, flowers or utensil holders for parties.

Figure 11.14. A turkey rack works well as a lid holder.

Source: S. Halbe.

Figure 11.15. Hanging pots and pans in an adjacent laundry room frees up space in the kitchen.

Source: C. Barry.

Colored or clear wine bottles can be used for water carafes.

Attractive illustrated empty cans be used to hold cooking tools, utensils, napkins and flowers or as an ice bucket for bottles of wine.

Store hanging pots and pans in the laundry room if you have available space on the walls and if it adjoins the kitchen area.

Figure 11.16. Labels on spices and condiments make interesting artwork.

Source: C. Barry.

ARTWORK IN THE KITCHEN

What do you do if there isn't enough wall space for artwork in the kitchen? No worries. You can advise your client that he already has a gallery of art in his kitchen, right there on his shelf. Here are some great ideas that Rose has put into use.

I use olive oil for most of my cooking needs. On occasion, I'll buy a large can of imported olive oil when it is beautifully illustrated. These oils are usually of very good quality and have distinctive flavors. At home I'll distribute them into smaller, manageable size bottles and store them in a cool dark place until I'm ready to use them. I've used these empty cans to hold cooking tools, flowers and chilled wine with ice. The artwork on many of these tins can be beautiful and creative.

One day, while setting up my kitchen, I started to line my bottles and cans of oils, paprika, salt and pepper onto the shelf next to my stove. As I wiped the surfaces of the bottles and tins clean, I turned them so their labels faced outward. In one of those Zen moments, my eyes became drawn to the colors and design of each container. Right in front of me were small pieces of art, each one telling a different story. These tins evoked a different mood, capturing my mind, heart, stomach and pocketbook.

Kitchen art had been hidden from me behind my pantry doors. Now that I had released them to the open shelf, my eyes were able to enjoy and appreciate them. I didn't need to buy paintings or art to decorate my kitchen. I had a gallery of little art pieces right on my shelves.

Another Discovery

When my husband and I lived in a rental Victorian flat, I was thrilled to find built-in cabinets with glass doors in the kitchen. The entire

Figure 11.17. The white backdrop of the cupboards provides a perfect frame for displaying colored dishes.

Source: C. Barry.

kitchen had been freshly painted a stark white. White walls, white cabinets, white drawers, white pantries all snowed under with this color.

I felt dismayed at this blizzard of whiteness. Then a lovely thing happened as I started stacking plates and bowls onto the shelves. To my delight, I started to notice that the white backdrop of the cupboards and shelves provided a perfect frame for my diversely colored bowls and plates. How was it that I hadn't noticed how colorful my eating utensils were?

This inspired me to line shelves over the sink and near the stove with oilcloth. Oh joy! I chose a pattern with multiple colored flowers that complimented the different colors of my cups and plates. My previously bland kitchen started to pop with color.

So much money and time is spent on product design in order to appeal to the consumer. On an unconscious level we are attracted to them and choose one product over the other based on how their labels appeal to us. Like the natural beauty that surrounds us every day, all too often our minds are elsewhere instead of right here in front of us. So, stop, open your eyes and look at all the beauty that's around you, especially labels, and use them to your advantage. And while your eyes are wide open, start looking at items on the market that are collapsible, foldable and adjustable that can serve to save you space.

## CHAPTER 12

ONE MAN'S TRASH IS ANOTHER'S TREASURE: COLLECTIBLES, ANTIQUES AND RECYCLED KNOWLEDGE

Figure 12.1. Recycled
items can be found at flea
markets.

Source: S. Halbe.

WAYS TO HELP YOUR CLIENT STAY WITHIN THEIR BUDGET AND BE SUSTAINABLE

Designers can help their clients find ways to recycle and stay within their budget. Rose presents ways to be both thrifty and sustainable.

Consignment Shops and Thrift Stores

There was a time, in the not too distant past, for some, when used items were considered shameful, a mark of low income. Individuals with limited financial resources and collectors of vintage goods were the only ones interested in these items.

Then the word recycling came into being and with it a growing awareness of the need for sustainability of our natural resources. The worldwide economic downturn has decreased the purchasing power of many people and the stigma of used and second-hand goods has transcended into an appreciation of collectibles, retro and, yes, vintage goods. Thrift shops and consignment stores for clothing and furniture have gained popularity in order to meet growing needs and interests.

Every used item holds a history. Each time an item exchanges hands it acquires another layer of memories. People let go of things for a variety of reasons. Some things are discarded because they are no longer functional while others are given to friends, family, charities or sold on consignment or to antique stores.

When looking for specific pieces, ask family and friends to keep an eye out for you. When I moved from my large house to a small condo I gave many of my kitchen wares, furniture and furnishings to friends. I gain a sense of pleasure whenever I see them in their new settings.

Most of the things sold in thrift stores range in quality from very good to good. Often times you can find almost new pieces of furniture. Finishes may be worn but everything must be functional. My daughter bought a mid-century, sturdy Danish-style wood dresser for $25 in San Francisco. She refinished it using an idea from a Pinterest article. I found a signed hand-thrown vase with a Persian motif and colors that had been converted into a lamp to hide the chip on its lip.

Figure 12.2. Vintage and retro treasures can be found at church or senior center sales.

Source: M. Rector Sanchez.

Tips for Purchasing at Consignment Shops

- **Find consignment shops that carry your style of furnishings and fit your price range.**
- **Form a relationship with the people who work at these shops.**
- **Check the stability of furniture.**
- **The price is determined by material, design and quality.**
- **Check to see if there is a tag with the mark down date.**
- **If the mark down date is close to when you want to purchase an item, ask if they will give you that discounted price.**

- **Always ask if they will sell it for the lower price.**
- **Be reasonable and fair about asking for discounts. Merchants also need to make money. Having a good relationship with a merchant may help with future purchases.**

Tips for Shopping in Thrift Stores

- **Check and make sure any upholstered furniture is free from stains, tears, worn spots and odors. Check under cushions and under and behind the frame for any problems.**
- **Check the stability of anything you buy. Some items may be functional but not necessarily stable. Sit on it and bounce around on it.**
- **Check wires on lamps and any electrical appliances to make sure they are secure and intact.**
- **Find out discount days. There are special days for seniors as well as non-seniors.**

Junk Yards

Goods sold in junk yards are often not as pretty or perfect but are almost always functional. They may need refinishing or may have a missing part that can be easily replaced. My gate-leg dining table cost only $75. The tabletop was water-marked but it was sturdy and had enough leaves to seat 12 people.

I constructed my office desk using a solid wood door supported by a set of two drawer file cabinets. I spray-painted the cabinets and door the same color and spent just $35 for everything.

Tips for Shopping at Junk Yards

- **When buying wood furniture, make sure the wood surface is solid and not peeling.**
- **Don't buy any wood furniture that is gouged unless you like that look.**
- **If you buy a table with leaves, put them in to see if they fit correctly.**
- **Sit in chairs and wiggle around. You want to make sure they are stable.**
- **If you buy any furniture that is made with a laminate, make sure the top is flat and not peeling. Check corners and edges for any curling or lifting.**
- **Be very careful with rattan furniture. Move pieces around to see if all the parts are tightly woven.**
- **Check rattan furniture for signs of infestation, mold and mildew odors.**

Websites

Craigslist and eBay are good online resources; however, it's hard to check the condition with a picture. Freecycle is a website where you can find things that are completely free! You'd be amazed at what people want to give away.

Free Furniture

It's amazing what people will throw out. My circa 1930s trestle table was rescued from a dumpster. It was a classic piece of furniture that just needed the top glued and secured. I found a seemingly brand new rattan chair with an immaculately clean cushion sitting on the sidewalk with a "For Free" sign on it. I'll never know the story behind why it was discarded but it's still in use after 15 years. I tend to be cautious of any upholstered furniture left outside. Make sure they are clean, unstained, no odors and in good condition.

The key to finding the specific pieces you are seeking is to first have a clear idea of what you are looking for. Go to stores, look through magazines and visit homes that are being staged for sale to get ideas. Once you decide upon the specific pieces you want, look over the room you will place it in and make a list of what colors, styles and sizes would work in that room. You may not find that perfect piece right away, but with a clear picture of what you want, your eyes will be attuned to seeing it when it crosses your path.

When choosing used furniture, keep in mind several things in making your choice. After finding a piece that fits your aesthetics needs, check for these main things.

- **Function – is it solid or unstable? If it is shaky, can you or someone strengthen it easily or affordably?**
- **How does it smell? If it smells funky of mildew or mold, pass on it.**
- **How is the finish? Can you refinish it or live with it with a covering?**
- **If the finish is trashed and can't be repaired easily, skip it.**

Wabi-Sabi

Not everything in your home has to be in perfect condition. There is a Japanese term called wabi-sabi. One meaning of the expression describes an appreciation for imperfections. I have two old sturdy mixing bowls that once belonged to my neighbor, Ruth. When she passed away her husband asked if I would like them. I prize them even though a piece of glaze is chipped off one and there's a

Figure 12.3. Wabi-sabi can be a chipped bowl filled with memories.

Source: C. Barry.

fine crack in the bowl section of the other. Every time I use them I remember and appreciate the sturdiness of my friendship with Ruth.

Other meanings of wabi-sabi are of eloquence, but not showy: an object that has simple aesthetic characteristics such as a wooden structure in a natural setting. Learn to appreciate those items that hold fond memories and use them with an appreciation of the beauty and history that lie within them.

COLLECTIBLES, ANTIQUES AND RECYCLED KNOWLEDGE: LESSONS FROM GRANDMA AND OTHER CULTURES

Collectibles and Antiques

Collectibles and antiques often work wonders in small quarters. Many times collectibles and even antiques can be relatively affordable. Collectibles are anything that one wants to collect. Antiques are

usually considered older. A trip to a shop or market that specializes in collectibles or antiques can give you a view into the past with usable solutions for small dwelling design. Furnishings and accessories are often smaller or have multifunctional, flexible and adjustable qualities.

Figure 12.4. Antique furnishings are often well made and add historical interest to a room.

Source: S. Halbe, Sonoma Country Antiques.

At the end of this chapter we have included a case study of a wonderful collectible and antique shop in Sonoma, California. Sonoma Country Antiques carries new and old furnishings and accessories, some of which have been finished and some that are in their original condition. Many of their wares can be used for functions other than the original purpose. An old French door might be used for a screen, as an example.

Some of the shop's accessories and furnishings have been procured from different countries. Perusing collectible and antiques establishments can be a good exercise in observing other cultures and the past in finding new and different design solutions.

Figure 12.5. Many antiques can be used for functions other than the original purpose.

Source: S. Halbe, Sonoma Country Antiques.

Figure 12.6. Chinese antiques displayed in this bathroom evoke a calm spiritual mood.

Source: R. Mark.

Recycled Knowledge

Recycling need not be limited to tangible items. We also recycle knowledge that we've learned from other people. In this day of ready-made fast foods, with too much to do and too little time, we often miss the opportunity to spend quality time with people from older generations and learn about domestic processes from other countries.

As mentioned before, it is important for interior designers to be aware that clients have different experiences, which influence their attitudes, values and needs. Designers need to consider their clients' social, cultural, economic, geographical and ecological backgrounds – or a global view – when analyzing their clients' needs.

For example, homemakers from our grandmothers' generation cooked from scratch and saved money by making good use of what they had on hand. You might ask how this information relates to interior design for small dwellings. When we design for our clients' routines, we need to make sure that we include fixtures or equipment that will accommodate specific functions. Younger generations may have been listening to the wisdom of past generations and have adopted their habits. Canning, making bone broth and fermentation are just some of these rediscovered ways of cooking.

Investigate your clients' cooking habits. Your client might need a different type of freezer or space for holding special equipment and food. Wine might require specific temperatures.

One of Sherrill's design students had a client who had a catering business and needed room for several pressure cookers. Luckily, the designer found space under a staircase and custom-designed a pantry that could store the equipment.

Another student worked with a client whose family members were vegans and needed kitchen storage and a processing space for cleaning daily farm vegetables. Past generations used cellars and cool closets to hold vegetables during the winter. Outdoor sinks were used for washing up after a hard day in the fields. Sherrill's student came up with an ingenious kitchen island that not only stored the fresh food, but kept the root vegetables and fruit well ventilated and colorfully displayed.

Figure 12.7. Antique or collectible stores can teach us about accessories of yesteryear.

Source: S. Halbe.

Figure 12.8. Consider how many ways you can use this ham.

Source: Hole Photography.

When designing small dwellings, we as designers can learn from past ways and other cultures in solving spatial and size-related problems. A trip to an antiques or collectibles store can teach us about very clever domestic furnishings, fixtures and equipment of yesteryear. Sherrill had an old built-in, flip-down ironing board in her flat in San

Francisco. Small dwellings, typical of the day, housed flexible furniture. An armoire or cabinet worked nicely for hanging clothing.

Always be alert to both old ideas and new examples of design possibilities from your local resources and from cultures around the world. Be aware of individual uniqueness and open your eyes to new solutions.

In the following vignette, Rose looks at generational habits, *New is Old and Old is New: A Few Things That Other Generations and Cultures Do to Save Money*, which illustrates past living practices that would require thoughtful design solutions. For example, the designer may need to include adequate freezer space or a special refrigerator compartment. The designer might also need to make room for drying herbs or storage for a colander and stock pot.

New is Old and Old is New: A Few Things That Other Generations and Cultures Do to Save Money

Older generations used every part of the roast. The carcass of a chicken or bones and tough parts of a roast were used to flavor stock. Bits and pieces of scrap meat often went into soups, stir fries, casseroles, fillings or hashes.

The freezer is a wonderful place to save those small pieces to make a dish for the following week. I stash my leftover chicken carcass or bones in the freezer to make a rich chicken stock. I save ends of bread to make a savory or sweet bread pudding. Leftover undressed pasta freezes well in a baggie and will defrost in a colander faster than cooking it up fresh. Use dry pasta or rice left in your cupboard and add them to a minestrone or chicken vegetable soup. Make a pan or pot of macaroni and cheese with all those little wedges of old cheese that's been sitting in your

---

frig. Just scrape or cut off any mold and add it to a cream sauce. Add some Dijon mustard, paprika and caramelized onion slices, combine with cooked pasta and, voila, you've got a unique dish.

Throw the stems of washed mushrooms into stock to give it a rich umami punch. Leftover carrots and celery from the crudité tray can be chopped up, sautéed until soft and frozen to add to stews, braises or soups.

Any fresh herbs that you know you won't be using can be dried on a surface that gets ventilation. Once dried, just put it in a little jar with a good lid. My favorite place to let herbs dry is over my mortar and pestle. It lends an inviting look to the kitchen.

These are just a few ideas of what grandmas and thrifty cooks have done through the ages. Start to look at the ingredients you use as parts of a whole and consider how many ways you can use them. You'll be surprised at how creative you can get and how much farther you can stretch your dollars. And don't forget to recycle the knowledge you've gained and give to someone else.

CASE STUDY 10: SONOMA COUNTRY ANTIQUES, SALES ASSOCIATE DESIGNER DIANE PORTELLO, SONOMA, CALIFORNIA, USA, 2017

Sonoma Country Antiques carries new and old furnishings and accessories, which have been acquired from France, England, Eastern Europe and Asia as well as accessories from India. Many of their collectibles and antiques can be used for different purposes and are multifunctional, working well in small spaces. Diane Portello, an Associate Designer for the store, advocates thinking outside the box and reimagining the possibilities of how you can turn a piece that you really love and makes a statement into furniture that serves

Figure 12.9. Think outside of the box by mixing antiques from different eras in a room.

Source: S. Halbe, Sonoma Country Antiques.

other uses. The important thing is to find something that speaks to you aesthetically and rethink its function.

You mentioned a personal story about how antiques have narratives and how your own vintage chest of drawers became even richer with a recent event.

I live in a small house and I purchased a great old antique chest of drawers, which I love. With each layer of paint, the 1870s piece was a favorite of mine and worked well in my home. After I acquired it a visitor's puppy also seemed to love it and gnawed a bit on the chest's wood. Rather than spoiling the chest, the story of an enamored little dog chewing the chest seemed to continue the chronicle of the chest. When you buy a collectible or antique, I think that the piece should draw you in with its story and you will add to it.

Figure 12.10. A collectible or antique should draw you in with its story.

Source: S. Halbe, Sonoma Country Antiques.

Figure 12.11. A large piece of furniture can be balanced with smaller items in a small room.

Source: S. Halbe, Sonoma Country Antiques.

You also have larger furnishings in your store. What are some of the ways you can make a small space seem spacious? Can you use a larger piece of furniture?

When you find furnishing that you really love, you can use a bigger piece with fewer small items. Creating a minimalistic look often reads spaciousness. Don't let a big chair or sofa put you off if you really like it. They can really make a space "feel bigger."

What about color, light and spaciousness?

People often stay away from black, thinking that it won't work in a small space. I like the idea of an accessory or type of furniture that is black with other colors. Black is a neutral and works well with other colors and woods.

And of course mirrors work well in small spaces. We carry many mirrors for the purpose of light, sparkle and the feel of spaciousness.

Figure 12.12. Creating a minimalistic look with larger furnishings often reads spaciousness.

Source: S. Halbe, Sonoma Country Antiques.

Figure 12.13. Black works well with other colors and woods.

Source: S. Halbe, Sonoma Country Antiques.

Figure 12.14. Mirrors work well in small spaces for the purpose of light, sparkle and the feel of spaciousness.

Source: S. Halbe, Sonoma Country Antiques.

Figure 12.15. Tie mixed woods together with other design attributes.

Source: S. Halbe, Sonoma Country Antiques.

How do you feel about mixing different kinds of woods or finishes together in a setting?

I mix wood all the time. You can tie furniture together with other design attributes; same with styles. A French antique is often stunning with a very modern design. You can create harmony or contrast by looking at other elements of the piece.

I see that the store carries a variety of hutches. What do you recommend to your clients about the use of a hutch?

You can repurpose a hutch to fit any need. You can use it to store anything from food to linens to clothing. Antiques often have little spaces that can be used successfully for your particular needs.

Do you have any tips on the use of furnishings in a bedroom?

In most rooms I like to see furniture placed asymmetrically. In bedrooms symmetry is nice in small spaces. With the bed in the middle, two end tables can be different pieces but similar lamps are nice to create symmetry and balance.

Any other advice for designers and their clients?

It is always helpful if the designer calls us before their trip to the store with their client. That way we can be more helpful if we have some idea of what is needed. Our store is intimate and personal but we really do have a big inventory housed within the shop's various rooms and a barn. We do personalized shopping as a service, too.

CHAPTER 13

LET ME ENTERTAIN YOU

Figure 13.1. Sharing food with another person is an act of love.

Source: C. Barry.

ENTERTAINING IN SMALL SPACES

A meaningful life includes people. When we connect with another person our life is enriched by the exchanges that take place. Whether it is with just one person or many, sharing of space, energy and thoughts contribute to our well-being.

Sharing food with another person is an act of love. It can be as simple as a cup of tea with buttered toast and jam or store-bought cookies. It can be as intimate as a supper or dinner party with four to six people or as lively as a gathering for 12 or more.

Food builds community. When we eat together we share and connect a part of ourselves through the exchange and enjoyment of the sight,

Figure 13.2. A meaningful
life includes people.

Source: S. Halbe, J. Ballou,
C. Hargrave.

smell and taste of what we partake. Tasty food is a social lubricant; it
can relax or energize people. It brings warmth into a home.

In this chapter we provide strategies for entertaining in a small
dwelling. With a greater understanding of the client's lifestyle, the
designer can provide solutions that lessen the stress of giving a
party by addressing specific entertaining needs, such as storage
space, furnishings, equipment or spatial challenges.

Using a participatory approach in design involves finding out about
the client's individual needs, wants and desires. Surveys are helpful
in programming and give the client the opportunity to think about
the questions, reflect and respond without being pressured. Their
responses provide the designer insight as to who they are. This information can then be used in a collaborative discussion to gain an
in-depth picture of what the client needs.

We start with the *Entertaining Questionnaire Example*, which is also provided in Appendix A. The designer can ascertain the degree of entertainment the client does by looking over this form. The information will aid in planning the design. Then, Rose will give helpful insight as to what she does when she entertains.

Entertaining Questionnaire Example

How many people are in your household?

My husband and myself

How often do you have people over for a meal?

Every month

What type of entertaining are you most comfortable doing? Please check your choices

Spontaneous   *x*

Take-out

Minimal Cooking   *x*

Involved Cooking   *x*

Planned   *x*

How many guest do you like to entertain? Please check your choices.

One, Two or Three   *x*

Four to Eight   *x*

Eight or More   *x*

What kind of parties do you like to give?

Formal

Cocktails and Appetizers   *x*

Dinner Parties   *x*

Breakfast or Brunch   *x*

Who likes to do the cooking?

I like to plan and cook but my husband helps

How comfortable are you at entertaining?

Not at All

Okay   *I need to be organized*

Very Comfortable

COMMON PROBLEMS AND SUGGESTIONS FOR ENTERTAINING

The following problems and suggestions are typical of giving parties, large or small. With years of experience, Rose provides you, the interior designer, a leg up with helpful tips that you can share with the client who wants to entertain in a small dwelling. Many of these suggestions exhibit awareness to dwelling requirements that need to be incorporated into the design. For example, the client may need

Figure 13.3. Use outdoor spaces to extend room for guests.

Source: C. Barry.

specific storage and counter space for preparation, supplies and work. You might ask similar questions to your client for insightful solutions.

Problems with Shortage of Space

I'd love to entertain more people but there isn't enough space in my house. I don't have enough chairs to seat more than six people.

Stress-Reducing Suggestions

- **Use outdoor space to extend room for guests.**
- **Throw large parties that don't require sitting, such as brunch or cocktail parties.**
- **Use your outdoor folding tables and chairs to accommodate more people.**
- **If you have adjoining living and dining rooms, use them to line up tables to accommodate larger sit-down affairs.**

Shortage of Space

Use any open area in front, behind and within your house such as decks, a yard or a garage to extend space for people to gather.

Set up small tables in rooms other than the main room where people can congregate. It can be as simple as a folding TV tray, card table, two sawhorses holding up a board or a cleared-off shelf. It's important to draw people to those areas so they know that space is available. Just put some food there and they'll get the idea. Simple snacks like a bowl of nuts or a dip with cut up vegetables or chips are easy and inviting.

This is an area where you don't have to spend much time. Once in a while you or a friend can check to see if anything needs replenishing. When guests bring snack items, direct them to put them on these small tables. Always make sure there is a bottle opener where beer or wine is being served.

Have a couple of chairs or stools around to provide some resting space. You don't need to provide a chair for each guest unless you're having a sit-down dinner. Often times at large parties, people circulate from room to room, rarely sitting down.

Figure 13.4. Napa Valley Deck Party.

Source: S. Halbe, P. and D. Bard, D. and F. Halbe, S. Halbe, D. Halbe, S. and G. Rector.

For large parties, set up your main food offerings on a table in the center of one room. This allows traffic to move around the table and encourages interaction and accessibility. This isn't as important in auxiliary rooms where you have snacks. Your main beverage station should be away from the food table. It can be in the same room but in a corner or on a deck, backyard or place people can easily find. Set up cups, openers and a starter set of beverages there. Put other beverages that need to be chilled outside or in any accessible spot away from food. Make sure you have wine and beer openers in those locations.

Big Party Challenges

I'd love to throw a big party but I don't have the space or budget.

Suggestions

- **Plan parties in which people do not have to sit.**
- **Use inside and outside spaces for guests.**
- **Time your party to fit your budget.**

Cocktail parties, brunches and late afternoon parties where most people mingle and move from space to space are great ways to entertain large groups. You don't need chairs for everyone at these casual affairs because your guests are eating and sitting at different times. The expense for a cocktail party will be higher than a brunch or afternoon party due to the cost of alcoholic beverages; however, there are different strategies to keep the cost down.

Once more, enlist the help of your friends to defray some of the cost of the liquor. You, however, must provide the starter rounds of drinks. Here are two approaches that my friends used in staying within a budget.

Figure 13.5. Use outdoor space for extending area for meal preparation, serving and seating.

Source: Michael Hospelt Photography, WEISBACH architecture | design, Gar Rector and Associates.

My writer friend, Erika, asked a few close friends to bring the makings for their favorite cocktail and prepare it for guests. Lively discussions were held around the mixing and making of these concoctions. In that way several types of cocktails were provided without Erika having to bear the cost. She provided wine, beer and non-alcoholic drinks as well as several appetizers.

Another friend, Sara, switched things around and provided three different types of mixed drinks, wine and non-alcoholic drinks as well as a few nibbles and small fresh tamales for later in the evening. She asked friends to bring wine and appetizers.

The overwhelming tasks for a party become simpler and more manageable when you organize the steps and break them down into parts that are done a little at a time.

Figure 13.6. Pull-out cutting boards provide additional counter and work space.

Source: R. Mark, K. Turcznski.

Organization makes a system of many appear fewer.
(Maeda 2015,ix)

OTHER DESIGN SOLUTIONS FOR ENTERTAINING USING MULTIFUNCTIONAL APPROACHES

The biggest challenge to entertaining in small dwellings is the shortage of counter space to prepare and serve drinks and food. Here are some solutions using multifunctional approaches.

Under-counter pull-out cutting boards can provide additional areas for preparing and holding prepared food. While typical kitchens have just one of these pull-out cutting boards, why not have several? They slip back under the counter when not needed.

Typical storage areas for baking sheets, racks and pans are vertically shaped. Designing a horizontal space for these tools with enough space between each shelf will enable the cook to store racks or pans with prepared food when needed. The same can be accomplished for under-counter use. Sliding shelves are always appreciated.

Rolling carts are often used to house wine and liquors for entertaining. A multiple shelf cart can be used for office purposes but can double to hold liquor and serving cart for drinks.

Finding additional spaces to set out food at large parties is a challenge for many people. Using fold-down tables, benches and nesting tables for everyday use provides adaptability when entertaining.

The outdoor area can provide additional space for entertaining. Storage chests for gardening tools can be used for additional seating or a table that is a flat and at a comfortable height.

Outdoor furnishings can be brought into the home if they are cleaned. Leveled flat outdoor spaces can be used as additional or permanent areas for entertaining.

Figure 13.7. Bring the outdoors inside using large windows facing plant life and nature.

Source: Libby Design Associates.

THE POWER OF INTERIOR DESIGN FOR SMALL DWELLING ENTERTAINMENT: LIBBY DESIGN ASSOCIATES' INNOVATIVE DESIGN SOLUTION FOR A DINING ROOM

Karen Libby, interior designer of Libby Design Associates, came up with an innovative design solution for her dining room. She turned an ordinary wall into a window case, which houses her collectible dinnerware on glass shelves and extends the room, visually, into her showcase garden. It is a space that fascinates

Figure 13.8. Karen's dining room before renovation.

Source: Libby Design Associates.

Figure 13.9. Karen's dining room after renovation.

Source: Libby Design Associates, © 2018 George Gruel.

the imagination and turns the room into an elegant vitrine. This place of entertainment exemplifies the power of interior design for small dwellings.

REFERENCE

Maeda, John. 2015. *The Laws of Simplicity.* Cambridge, MA: MIT Press.

SMALLER, SIMPLER, RICHER: A PHILOSOPHY

In this book we present ways that have been successful for us, offering designers a teaching guide and a practical manual in designing small dwelling. We have embedded a philosophy throughout our book, based on the power of simplicity, sustainability and connectivity. By simplifying our lives and dwellings we can recognize what is important to us and validate who we are.

This Epilog reiterates our philosophy, summarizes the benefits of living small and concludes with current thought on the value of participatory and inclusive design methodology in obtaining this end. Designers can partake in this exciting avenue of sustainable practice for clients who are ready to build environments that support a healthy planet and individual values.

Clients often express concern and anxieties about interior design issues such as color or budget. Assurance and support on these issues can be achieved by sharing information in the form of talk, articles or written strategies. Using a participatory approach in design involves finding out about the client's individual needs and dreams. We have provided thought-provoking tools in the form of questionnaires and exercises throughout the book. These forms allow the client the opportunity to think about the questions, reflect and respond without being pressured. Their responses provide the designer a beginning picture of who they are. This information can then be used in a collaborative discussion to gain a more in-depth picture of what the client wants.

We don't think that living in a small space means living small. We believe that by simplifying our lives intelligently and applying certain principles of design, planning and organization, we can live a deeper, richer and more satisfying life. We can build our environments to support our individual values and gain empowerment in the process. We can establish a sense of place; a deep inner feeling of where we belong. As expressed from *A Gentleman in Moscow*,

This efficiency of design was music to the young mind. It attested to a precision of purpose and the promise of adventure... And wouldn't any young boy with the slightest gumption gladly trade a hundred nights in a palace for one aboard the *Nautilus*?

(Towles 2016, 15)

We have included some quotes from our friends and clients who live in small dwelling; ordinary people who have enjoyed the rewards that echo our experiences and philosophy. We invite you to join us.

By living in a 600 square feet home my husband and I have learned to respect each other's space while at the same time sharing time and place, face to face.

Every time we think about buying something new for the house we go through the exercise of asking ourselves where we will store it, can it serve several purposes and will we really use it. We save a lot of money going through this process.

We have everything within finger reach, more or less.

Our heating bill is much more reasonable and the house is always warm and cozy.

Our small home is easier to clean, which frees up more time to do what I want to do.

We are like two peas in a pod and it always feels good to come home.

Figure 14.1. Mesa Verde National Park. Form and function in an ancient dwelling.

Source: S. Halbe.

REFERENCE

Towles, Amor. 2016. *A Gentleman in Moscow.* New York, NY: Viking. 14.

RESOURCES

EXERCISES AND WORKSHEETS

PART 1 ANALYZING YOUR CLIENT'S NEEDS

Exploring the Client's Living Situation
Daily Routine Worksheet for the Client
Inventory of Furnishings and Accessories for the Client
  and Designer
Essential, Desired and Future Needs for the Client
Physical Interior Elements for the Client
Physical Interior Characteristics for the Designer
Building in Context for the Client
Building in Context for the Designer
What Function Does each Room Provide For the Client?
Aesthetic Desires for the Client
Universal, Accessible, Aging in Place and Healthy
  Environmental Design for the Client
Budget and Scheduling for the Client

EXPLORING THE CLIENT'S LIVING SITUATION

Example

List characteristics about who you are and your related needs. For example, interview yourself and write down your age, socioeconomic status, community needs and physical conditions including if you are right- or left-handed and if you have vision or hearing needs. If you have other family members, write down the same characteristics for them. Do you live in a multigenerational household?

Jane, age 53, female; semi-retired; active in gardening, yoga and running; volunteer work; nearsighted; left-handed;

Exercise

1. List characteristics about who you are and your related needs.

2. Ask yourself where you would like to live.

3. List values that matter to you.

4. How do you feel about privacy, personalized space, control of space, territoriality, order, variety, aesthetics, socialization with friends and family cohesiveness?

5. Consider when you can put a plan in place.

DAILY ROUTINE WORKSHEET FOR THE CLIENT

Example

AM

turn off alarm clock, walk dog, toilet, shower, use lotions on body, put on makeup, put on tea kettle, make tea/coffee, eat breakfast, clean up, run errands or work at laptop.

Exercise

AM

Midday

PM

INVENTORY OF FURNISHINGS AND ACCESSORIES FOR THE CLIENT AND DESIGNER

What do you have in each room? List the number, description, color and material of each furnishing and accessory that you have in each room. **The designer can add dimensions and other characteristics to this form later. Please note if a lighting fixture is moveable or stationary. See examples in Chapter 3.

Example

Furnishings and Accessories in the Living Room

#	Description	Color	Material	**W, H, D	Other
1	Chaise Sofa	Green	Velveteen		
1	Sofa Bed	White	Cloth		
1	Bertoia Chair	White	Cloth		

Exercise

Furnishings and Accessories in the Living Room

#	Description	Color	Material	**W, H, D	Other

Furnishings and Accessories in the Dining Room

#	Description	Color	Material	**W, H, D	Other

Furnishings and Accessories in the Kitchen

#	Description	Color	Material	**W, H, D	Other

Furnishings and Accessories in the Bedroom

#	Description	Color	Material	**W, H, D	Other

Furnishings and Accessories in the Bedroom

#	Description	Color	Material	**W, H, D	Other

Furnishings and Accessories in the Bathroom

#	Description	Color	Material	**W, H, D	Other

ESSENTIAL, DESIRED AND FUTURE NEEDS FOR THE CLIENT

Think of all of your household needs even if they seem impossible to realize in a small space. Every square inch counts so there are ways to accommodate what is important to you. Arrange your list by priorities as to what is essential and what is desired. Prioritize what is needed now and what you will need in the future.

Example

Bedroom

Essential needs	Desired Needs	Future Needs
Chair(s)	*Armoire*	*Ottoman*

Exercise

Write down what you must have in each room under the essential needs section first, then fill in the desired needs and finally add future needs.

Living Room

Essential Needs	Desired Needs	Future Need

Dining Room

Essential Needs	Desired Needs	Future Needs

Kitchen

Essential Needs	Desired Needs	Future Needs

Bedroom

Essential Needs	Desired Needs	Future Needs

Bedroom

Essential Needs	Desired Needs	Future Needs

Bathroom

Essential Needs	Desired Needs	Future Needs

PHYSICAL INTERIOR ELEMENTS FOR THE CLIENT

Look at your existing dwelling and its physical interior elements such as lighting, outlets, windows, doors, and structural and non-structural partitions. Write down physical interior elements that you might like to change.

Example

Bedroom

Possible Changes

Two outlets on each wall

Sliding doors instead of closet with swinging doors

Exercise

Living Room

Possible Changes

Dining Room

Possible Changes

Kitchen

Possible Changes

Bedroom

Possible Changes

Bedroom

Possible Changes

Bathroom

Possible Changes

PHYSICAL INTERIOR CHARACTERISTICS FOR THE DESIGNER

Example

Bedroom

Existing

1 outlet on each of the four walls

Possible Changes

Two outlets on each wall

Exercise

Living Room

Existing

Possible Changes

Dining Room

Existing

Possible Changes

Kitchen

Existing

Possible Changes

Bedroom

Existing

Possible Changes

Bedroom

Existing

Possible Changes

Bathroom

Existing

Possible Changes

BUILDING IN CONTEXT FOR THE CLIENT

For your existing dwelling, take note of all of its physical exterior elements. Include things like: sun orientation (what side of the house gets the morning sun?), natural settings and accessibility to the outdoors, climate orientation (what's the weather like?), scenery, etc.

Take note of those characteristics. Write down what you like and what might be changed.

Example

First of all, what places in nature are you drawn to? Places like mountains, water, parks, forest, woods?

I love the mountains and water

Exercise

What places in nature are you drawn to? Places like mountains, water, parks, forest, woods?

How do you feel about sustainability? What are your needs?

Tell about the outside of your home:

Sun orientation (what side of the house gets the morning sun?)

Natural settings and accessibility to the outdoors

Climate orientation – what's the weather like?

Scenery

Urban, suburban, rural setting
Noise levels

Style or characteristic of the exterior of your home

BUILDING IN CONTEXT FOR THE DESIGNER

Take note of additional contextual elements. Include sun orientation, natural settings and accessibility to the outdoors, climate orientation, etc.

Exercise

Exterior of building, style, materiality, etc.

Sun orientation

Natural settings and accessibility to the outdoors

Climate orientation

Views

Urban, suburban, rural setting

Noise levels

Other characteristics

WHAT FUNCTION DOES EACH ROOM PROVIDE FOR THE CLIENT?

Each room serves physical and emotional functions. What do you want to do in that room? What kind of feelings do you want to have in this room?

Example

Bedroom

Physical   *Sleep, rest, watch TV, read*

Emotional   *A place to sleep and relax. A quiet, soothing place; a place to get away from activity*

Exercise

Living Room

Physical

Emotional

Dining Room

Physical

Emotional

Kitchen

Physical

Emotional

Bedroom

Physical

Emotional

Bedroom

Physical

Emotional

Bathroom

Physical

Emotional

AESTHETIC DESIRES FOR THE CLIENT

Think about your fantasies and what might give you emotional satisfaction. The aesthetics of color, texture and shapes can express themselves in fabric, furnishings and architectural detail. Here is a worksheet for expressing your desires for each room. Fill out the name of each room you are describing on a separate sheet. Feel free to make additional copies of this worksheet in the event you run out of space.

Example

Bedroom

I've always wanted

A barn door divider

I dream about these objects, furniture, architectural details in my environment

Silk table skirt

What colors spring to mind in this room?

Dusty rose

Creamy warm off-white

Exercise

Living Room

I've always wanted

I dream about these objects, furniture architectural details in my environment

What colors spring to mind in this room?

Dining Room

I've always wanted

I dream about these objects, furniture architectural details in my environment

What colors spring to mind in this room?

Kitchen

I've always wanted

I dream about these objects, furniture architectural details in my environment

What colors spring to mind in this room?

Bedroom

I've always wanted

I dream about these objects, furniture architectural details in my environment

What colors spring to mind in this room?

Bedroom

I've always wanted

I dream about these objects, furniture architectural details in my environment

What colors spring to mind in this room?

Bathroom

I've always wanted

I dream about these objects, furniture architectural details in my environment

What colors spring to mind in this room?

UNIVERSAL, ACCESSIBLE, AGING IN PLACE AND HEALTHY ENVIRONMENTAL DESIGN FOR THE CLIENT

Do you have any specific needs to be included in your design for now or the future? Do you have allergies or sensitivities to types of flooring, materials or lighting? Do you have or will you need additional space requirements for medical equipment? Do you need special hardware for present or future health needs?

Example

I am allergic or sensitive to these types of building materials.

I am sensitive to fluorescent light. The fumes from most paints and certain flooring materials affect my respiratory system.

Exercise

I am allergic or sensitive to these types of building material

I need or will need aging-in-place hardware on doors, cabinets and other fixtures

I need or will need additional space for medical equipment.

BUDGET AND SCHEDULING FOR THE CLIENT

Think about a realistic budget. What monies do you have available now and what might you have in the future? You don't need to purchase everything at the same time. Take time to explore the type of furniture or accessory that will fit in with your dream design. The clearer you are in knowing what you want, the easier it will be to find it. Prioritize what items you want to purchase new and what you are open to buying second hand. This will save you money.

Example

What is the scope of your project?

I want to choose furnishings and flooring for my new condo.

Exercise

What is the scope of your project?

What is your spending range for your project as you see it now?

Do you have accessible money for your project?

Will you have future funds for your project?

Are you willing to do your project in phases or do you want to do it all at once?

Based on the information that we have obtained from the other exercises, what would you want to do now? What is your time frame?

Based on the information that we have obtained from other exercises, when would you want to implement future plans?

When you choose your furnishings, fixtures, equipment, materials and finishes will you spend more for function, sustainability or how it looks?

When you choose your furnishings, fixtures, equipment, materials and finishes do you want to stay in a high, mid or low price range?

When you choose your furnishings, fixtures, equipment, materials and finishes do you want to consider quality over a set price range?

If you are trying to stay in a certain range are you okay with a mix of high, mid and low end items?

If you have an amount in mind are you willing to look at options out of your price range?

Are you willing to look at options below your price range?

PART 2 DESIGN CONSIDERATIONS

Observing Design in Nature Exercise for the Client

Adventures and Exercises in Learning to "See" Colors – a
Checklist or Place for Notes

A Color Exercise for a "Room of One's Own" For
the Client

Color Association for the Client Exercise

Space Planning Checklist and Worksheet for the
Designer

OBSERVING DESIGN IN NATURE

The following exercise illustrates the interaction between elements and principles of design, which creates a means of expression. In *Observing Design in Nature* you will utilize and imitate nature to find creative ideas for your designs.

Take a walk, sit in nature or gaze out of a window. This is a nice way to open your eyes to design in nature and will help you identify the parts and characteristics of design.

OBSERVING DESIGN IN NATURE EXERCISE FOR THE CLIENT

Design is all around us. Observe nature and only think of what you see and tune into your other senses. How does the experience make you feel? Keep other thoughts on hold while you only use your eyes, ears, nose and skin. Remember you are looking for the following elements and principles in nature:

Example

I am attracted to a winter morning scene from my window. I can use this color palette for my client who desires blue for her bedroom, but doesn't want it to appear too cold. This scene illustrates warmth of the ground colors with a variety of blue tints and shades from the sky and the background trees.

Elements of Design

Line

Shape

Space

Texture and pattern

Color – value, tint, shade, intensity, neutrals

Light

Principles of Design

Harmony and unity
Repetition and rhythm
Movement
Contrast
Variety
Emphasis/accent
Balance

Write about what you see in nature in this space. You might also sketch or take photos of areas that really speak to you.

ADVENTURES AND EXERCISES IN LEARNING TO "SEE" COLORS – A CHECKLIST OR PLACE FOR NOTES

1. As we did before when we discussed the elements and principles of design, look at color in nature. Take a walk or sit in the mountains or park and try to do nothing but walk or sit, enjoy the day and look at the subtleties of the tiniest and largest parts of nature.

2. Keep a folder of magazine photos or photographs that you take of interiors that really, really attract you.

3. Gather color samples of paint chips, fabric, tile, wood, etc. and keep a color collection of items you love. Make a color material board by gluing samples for a room on poster board.

4. Keep your eye alert to visual advertisements of clothing, products and art that attract your attention. Visit art shows and keep visual records of pieces that inspire passion.

A COLOR EXERCISE FOR A "ROOM OF ONE'S OWN" FOR THE CLIENT

Example

The flooring is yellowish salmon colored tiles with beige grout. The fireplace is brushed nickel with black trim. I want to keep the dark brown leather settee.

Exercise

1. The first step is to really look at the materials and furnishings that will stay in the room. Everything has color with the exception of black, gray, and white and these neutrals are part of the color palette. Train your eye to see the black–red in brick, the blue–gray in stone, and the brownish-gold of wood flooring. Get samples, if you can, and add them to a color material collection.

2. Secondly, take note of the room's lighting sources such as windows and artificial lighting. Note the orientation of natural light such as northern exposure or the filtering of light from outdoor foliage or indoor window treatment. Do you have a view? Views have color.

5. Next, note the areas of the room that will require color such as walls, floors, ceilings, trim, window treatment, doors, windows, built-ins, lighting fixtures and furnishings. Don't forget hardware such as door knobs and handles, accessories, and artwork.

6. Now, have some fun, and think about the kind of atmosphere you want to create in your room: Is it a calm and restful room or stimulating and playful? Perhaps it is refined and dignified or just laid back. Write down the colors that might lend themselves to this atmosphere. You might want to do some of the following exercises for inspiration before doing this part.

COLOR ASSOCIATION FOR THE CLIENT EXERCISE

Write down the first thing you what you think about when you read or hear a name of a color. Don't think too hard or long – just the first thing that comes to mind. There is no right or wrong answer but you will see how your response to a color might have psychological, sociological or cultural associations.

Example

Red   *Bright, hot, exciting*

Exercise

Red	Red–Orange
Blue	Blue–Green
Yellow	Yellow–Green
Violet	Red–Violet
Green	Black
White	Blue–Violet
Orange	Yellow–Orange
Gray	Brown

SPACE PLANNING CHECKLIST AND WORKSHEET FOR THE DESIGNER

Check the following:

1. _____ At the entrance have you provided enough space for physical movement and psychological transition from the outside of the home to the inside of the home?

2. _____ View from the entrance – is there an inviting view of what is beyond and within the area?

3. _____ Daylight and views – check out window light and views and consider what rooms would benefit or not from light, heat and outside views.

4. _____ Building structure – are there potential obstacles in room shapes and details? For example, long rectangular rooms, high or low ceilings, posts, or narrow hallways.

5. _____ Public and private areas – figure out ways to screen and accommodate personal areas from group areas.

6. _____ Workable space – figure out the best place where the kitchen, bathroom, living room, etc. will function.

7. _____ Areas that need to be next to each other – place areas convenient to one another, such as the eating area close to the kitchen or the bathroom near the bedroom.

8. _____ Circulation within the spaces – provide enough space for physical movement and psychological transition from one space to another.

9.   _____Furniture layout – think about spaces for entertainment; number of family members and their activities.

10.   _____Circulation within seating areas – provide enough space for movement, sitting down comfortably and traffic paths within and outside of the seating area.

11.   _____Sounds and smells – consider acoustical and odor problems and solutions from the outside and within.

12.   _____Space to accommodate wheelchairs and special equipment.

PART 3 PRACTICAL SOLUTIONS FOR LIVING WELL IN A SMALL DWELLING

KITCHEN USE QUESTIONNAIRE FOR THE CLIENT

Example

1. How many people typically cook in the kitchen?

My husband and I take turns cooking. Occasionally, we both cook at the same time. On the weekends the kids cook with us.

Exercise

1. How many people typically cook in the kitchen?

2. How often does someone cook in your kitchen?

Breakfast

Lunch

Dinner

3. Do you or anyone in your household need any space, material or height considerations in the kitchen?

4. What types of food and/or items do you consider staples in your kitchen?

5. How often do you entertain guests?

6. Do you include your guests in the kitchen or do you entertain them in another room?

7. Will you use the kitchen space for other activities?

8. Would you rather have an open kitchen to the other rooms or a kitchen that is enclosed?

KITCHEN APPLIANCES AND TOOLS: HOW MANY DO YOU HAVE AND HOW MANY DO YOU NEED? AN EXERCISE FOR THE CLIENT

What kitchen equipment do you have or plan to acquire? Consider appliances that are convenient and ergonomically functional. We have provided exercises with examples.

Example

Please list each kitchen appliance and check how often you use it.

Appliance	Daily	Weekly	Monthly	Yearly	Once in a Blue Moon
Mixer	*x*				

Exercise

Please list each kitchen appliance and check how often you use it.

Appliance	Daily	Weekly	Monthly	Yearly	Once in a Blue Moon

PURCHASING INVENTORY EXERCISE FOR THE CLIENT

Every kitchen is as individual as the people who use it. What is your life in the kitchen?

Example

1.   What type of food do you and your family eat weekly?

We eat simple fast breakfasts such as eggs, yoghurt and fruit.

We eat sandwiches or leftovers for lunch.

We love to cook foods from different cultures that concentrate on lots of vegetables and grains with small amounts of meat.

Exercise

What type of food do you and your family eat weekly?

How much meat, poultry, fish, dairy, grains or beans do you eat?

What items do you buy each week?

What ingredients do you typically use each week or month?

How many meals do you cook during the week?

Which meal do you cook the most?

What types of meals do you cook, such as Italian, Chinese, Latin, Indian or Middle Eastern?

PURCHASING EXERCISE FOR THE CLIENT

Here's an exercise that can help you organize and plan your food purchases. We have provided an example and an exercise.

Example

Make a list of each meal you prepare or serve daily. Write down what you serve during the week for each meal. Then write down the ingredients you need to prepare these meals.

Breakfast   *Cold cereal, toast, eggs or take out*

Lunch Bring lunch or eat out

Dinner   *Fast food, ready-made food or prepared meals*

Exercise

Make a list of each meal you prepare or serve daily. Write down what you serve during the week for each meal. Then write down the ingredients you need to prepare these meals.

1. Typical meal for weekday

2. Typical meal for weekend

3. Number of items needed to make weekly meals

ENTERTAINING QUESTIONNAIRE FOR THE CLIENT

This information will aid in planning for entertainment in the design.

Example

How many people are in your household?

My husband and myself

Exercise

How many people are in your household?

How often do you have people over for a meal?

What type of entertaining are you most comfortable doing? Please check your choices.

How many guests do you like to entertain? Please check your choices.

What kind of parties do you like to give?

Who likes to do the cooking?

How comfortable are you at entertaining?

PROGRAM TEMPLATE FOR THE DESIGNER

PROGRAM TEMPLATE FOR THE DESIGNER

After you have analyzed your client's needs and filled in the Program Exercises, you can combine the exercises with the following Program Template to keep a concise record of what you want to pay attention to when you design their home. You can also refer to our sample program, *Rose's Phoenix Commons Design Program* in the Appendix, and see how we utilized this template.

Owners

Name

Summarized description of owners:

Name/Site Address

Summarized description of property:

Existing Physical Characteristics

THE MEASURING RECORD SHEET

The following format is for recording physical information about the client's rooms. Make copies of this template for each room in the home

Room			
Measurement Record Sheet	Width	Length	Height
Floor--Width and Length			
Walls--Width and Height			
North			
South			
East			
West			
Doors--Width and Height			

Width from the Corner of the Room to the Door Opening			
Windows--Width and Height			
Width from the Corner of the Room to the Window Opening			
Heights--Floor to Window Sill			
Indicate Window's Natural Light Direction: North, South, West or East			
Indicate if the Window Opens			
Built-in Features such as Cabinetry--Width and Height			
Height of Built-in Features to the Ceiling			
Width from the Corner of the Room to Built-in Features			

PHYSICAL ROOM CHARACTERISTICS

The following format is for recording physical information about the client's rooms. Make copies of this template for each room in the home

Room
Physical Room Characteristics
Existing Material/Finishes of Building that Can't be Changed. **Example: Brick Fireplace**
Walls
Flooring
Ceiling
Doors
Windows

Built-in Features and Finishes such as Cabinetry
Other Elements and Materials such as a White Brick Fireplace

LIGHTING AND ELECTRICAL

The following format is for recording physical information about the client's rooms. Make copies of this template for each room in the home

Room	
List Fixed Lighting Sources Such as Recessed, Fixture or Sconce	
Number and Placement of Outlets and Light Switches:	
Indicate Placement such as the West Wall	**Number**

Other Information Regarding Lighting	
Lighting and Electrical Record	

SUPPLIES, EQUIPMENT RECORD AND STORAGE PLACEMENT INFORMATION

The following format is for Recording Supplies, Equipment and Storage Placement Information. Make copies of this template for each room in your home.

Room	
Supplies/Equipment Record and Storage/Placement Information	
Supplies/Equipment	**Storage/ Placement**
Supplies/Equipment Record and Storage/ Placement Information	

DESIGN PROGRAM: ROSE'S CONDOMINIUM PROGRAM

DESIGN PROGRAM: ROSE'S CONDOMINIUM PROGRAM

Owners

Owners: Rose Mark and Larry Beresford

Condo

Residence: Phoenix Commons: A Senior Cooperative Lifestyle Community on the Oakland Waterfront

Site Address: 340 29th Avenue, Oakland, CA 9460

1 Bed/1 Bath, 624 square feet space (57.97 square meters)

Phoenix Commons is a LEED-certified co-op building for active 55+ residents. The units are individually owned and include shared ownership interest in common spaces such as community rooms. The building is designed for aging in place and equipped with emergency call and security systems.

The owners, Rose and Larry are active, curious, professional writers who like to entertain, cook, read, walk the dog, listen to music, watch movies and enjoy community life. The couple wants an interior that accommodates and reflects their life styles and personalities. Rose explains, "I want my living environment to reflect who I am as well as meet my physical needs/limitations for now and the future. I'm on a fixed income with a small budget for home improvement and I want to use as much of what I already have rather than purchase new furniture."

The Condo's Existing Physical Characteristics

Rose and Larry's home consists of a kitchen with dining area, a living room, a bedroom with two closets and a bathroom. Other facilities in the four-story building include two elevators, a communal laundry room, kitchen, dining room, three lounges, library, office and a first-floor atrium with a hot tub.

Interior Measurements and Information

Bedroom and Hall

Approximately 170 square feet (15.79 square meters); W 11 feet 1 inch (3.38 meters) × L 15 feet 4 inches (4.67 meters) × H 9 feet 0 inches (2.74 meters) floor to ceiling; hall and closet space approximately 33 square feet (3.06 square meters); room approximately 132 square feet (12.26 square meters).

Total of 624 square feet (57.97 square meters).

Northwest wall, W 15 feet 4 inches (4.67 meters) × H 9 feet 0 inches (2.74 meters).

Northeast wall, W 11 feet 1 inches (3.38 meters) × H 9 feet 0 inches (2.74 meters).

Southeast wall, W 15 feet 4 inches (4.67 meters) × H 9feet 0 inches (2.74 meters).

Southwest wall, W 11 feet 1 inches (3.38 meters) × H 9 feet 0 inches (2.74 meters).

Door: W 3 feet 0 inches (.91 meters) × H 7 feet 0 inches (2.13 meters), conventional swing in, painted red–orange.

Door is on the southwest wall, 6 feet (1.83 meters) from southeast wall corner, right hinge.

Window: W 7 feet 0 inches (2.13 meters) × H 3 feet 0 inches (.91 meters); 2 feet 6 inches (.76 meters) sill height (floor to window sill); casement, push-out left hinge; right side fixed; northwest light exposure; W 3 feet 6 inches (1.07 meters) from corner of the northeast wall to the window opening.

Closet: 7 feet 1 inch (2.16 meters) × 3 feet 4 inches (1.02 meters) interior space.

Closet on southwest wall, floor to ceiling, sliding doors.

Existing off-white walls and ceiling – Benjamin Moore Mayonnaise; custom color to be determined – possibly blue.

Flooring, Mammoth, Marmoleum over acoustic concrete.

Living Room

Approximately 170 square feet (15.98 square meters); W 12 feet 8.5 inches (3.88 meters) × L 11 feet 11.5 inches (3.66 meters); H 9 feet 0 inches (2.74 meters) floor to ceiling.

Northeast wall, W 11 feet 11.5 inches (3.66 meters) × H 9 feet 0 inches (2.74 meters).

Southeast wall, W 12 feet 8.5 inches (3.88 meters) × H 9 feet 0 inches (2.74 meters).

Southwest wall, W 11 feet 11.5 inches (3.66 meters) × H 9 feet 0 inches (2.74 meters).

Window is on the southeast wall: approximately W 6 feet 4 inches (1.96 meters) × H 3 feet 0 inches (.91 meters); 2 feet 6 inches (.76 meters) sill height; casement, push-out left hinge; right side fixed; southeast light exposure; W 6 feet 4.5 inches (1.96 meters) from corner of the southwest wall to the window opening.

The kitchen peninsula is 8 feet 0 inches (2.43 meters) W and perpendicular to the southwest wall, dividing the living room from the kitchen.

Existing off-white walls and ceiling – Benjamin Moore Mayonnaise on the northeast, southeast and southwest wall.

Flooring, Mammoth Marmoleum flooring over acoustic concrete.

Kitchen/Dining Room/Entrance

Entry into Kitchen

Approximately 172 square feet (15.98 square meters); W 12 feet 8.5 inches (3.88 meters) × L 13 feet 6.5 inches (4.14 meters) × H 9 feet 0 inches (2.74 meters) floor to ceiling.

Northwest wall, W 12 feet 8.5 inches (3.88 meters) × H 9 feet 0 inches (2.74 meters).

Northeast wall, W 13 feet 6.5 inches (4.14 meters) × H 9 feet 0 inches (2.74 meters).

Southwest wall, W 13 feet 6.5 inches (4.14 meters) × H 9 feet 0 inches (2.74 meters).

Door: W 3feet 0 inches (.91 meters) × H 7 feet 0 inches (2.13 meters), swing in French door, the frame is painted red–orange.

Door is on the northwest wall, 6 feet (1.83 meters) from northeast wall corner, right hinge.

Window: W 4 feet 0 inches (1.22 meters) × H 3 feet 0 inches (.91 meters); 2 feet 6 inches (.76 meters) sill height; casement, push-out left hinge; right side fixed; northwest light exposure; W 4 feet 0 inches (1.22 meters) from corner of the northeast wall to the window opening.

Built-in kitchen cabinets on southwest wall; cabinet W 12 feet 0 inches (3.66 meters); H 7 feet 0 inches (2.13 meters); 2 feet 0 inches (.60 meters) from top of cabinets to ceiling.

Rose will use the unused top space to display and store vases and large platters.

There will not be any pull-out shelves. Rose is planning to install pull-out shelves on bottom shelves.

The kitchen peninsula is 8 feet 0 inches (2.43 meters) W and perpendicular to the southwest wall, dividing the living room from the kitchen.

Existing off-white walls and ceiling – Benjamin Moore Mayonnaise; custom color to be determined for walls, possibly saffron backsplash.

Cabinet style and finish: slab doors, light maple finish.

Cabinet hardware: handles (aging-in-place) style and finish to be determined.

Sink: style, size, color and fixture finish and style to be determined. Fixture handles meet universal standards.

Countertop: granite – mottled black, gray, off-white.

Backsplash: granite – mottled black, gray, white cove; off-white painted wall.

Stove, oven, microwave, dishwasher and refrigerator: stainless steel; appliances cannot be moved; vent over stove with fan.

Rose and Larry will use the free communal laundry area, which will allow space in their condo.

Bathroom

Approximately 70 square feet. (6.50 square feet); W 7 feet 2 inches (2.18 meters) × 9 feet 3 inches (2.82 meters); H 8 feet 0 inches (2.43 meters) floor to ceiling.

Northwest wall, W 7 feet 2 inches (2.18 meters) × H 9 feet 0 inches (2.74 meters).

Northeast wall, W 9 feet 3 inches (2.82 meters) × H 9 feet 0 inches (2.74 meters).

Southeast wall, W 7 feet 2 inches (2.18 meters) × H 9 feet 0 inches (2.74 meters).

Southwest wall, W 9 feet 3 inches (2.82 meters) × H 9 feet 0 inches (2.74 meters).

Door: W 3 feet 0 inches (.91 meters) × H 7 feet 0 inches (2.13 meters), pocket door, painted – color to be determined.

Door is on the northwest wall, 6 feet (1.83 meters) from southwest wall corner.

Existing off-white walls and ceiling – Benjamin Moore Mayonnaise.

Cabinet style and finish: slab doors, light maple finish.

Cabinet hardware: handles (aging-in-place style and finish).

Sink: style, size, color and fixture finish and style to be determined. Fixture handles meet universal standards.

Countertop: granite – mottled black, gray, off-white.

Backsplash: granite – mottled black, gray, white cove; white painted wall.

Flooring: Mammoth, Marmoleum over acoustic concrete.

One standard size towel rack, one smaller towel rack, one vanity mirror, lighting, storage, mirror on medicine cabinet.

Lighting and Electricity

4 Recessed LED ceiling lights in each room.

Under-counter LED lighting in kitchen.

Outlets on each wall of each room except bathroom.

Bathroom outlets on east and west wall and near sink.

BUILDING, EQUIPMENT AND FIXTURE INFORMATION

Walls are standard, double stud with air space, 6 inches (.15 meters) space between walls.

Stove hoods will be recirculating and flow through the ventilator.

Windows will have sound-deadening windows.

Z ducts air ducts baffle sound vertical chamber.

Bathroom fan will be used to draw air into the unit.

All rooms except bathroom will have operable windows.

Power source: solar panels will provide community use of hot water.

Power source for stove, refrigerator and heating for individual units will be electric.

Gas stoves on first-floor communal kitchen.

All units are wired with internet connection.

Landline for all phones will be connected through internet.

PARTIAL PROGRAMMING SUMMARIES OBTAINED FROM EXERCISES IN THIS BOOK

Owners' Functional Needs and Desires

Bedroom

A place for rest and retreat that needs to be calming and peaceful.

General Needs

Room for a queen-sized bed
Lighting for reading
Dressing room
Clothes closet
Storage for personal needs
Room for books, radio
Privacy
Quiet
Window covering for privacy and to block out or filter sun
Shelving for books, clothes
Storage space for seasonal clothes, blankets
End tables or two multifunctional chairs to hold two
    CPAP machines and one clock

Bedroom Desires

Bed with shelves under platform
Closet with double deck rack with shelving units
End tables or two multifunctional chairs

Entrance

When I enter my dwelling, I want to see a room that
reflects the creative energy/artists that Larry and I are

I want the colors, shapes and objects in the rooms to
express our curiosity and love of life

I want the walls in the entrance, living room or dining
area to be a Moroccan red

I want the backsplash areas in the kitchen to be a
mustardy yellow or any rich yellow that complements
that theme

Living Room

General Needs

Sufficient seating for at least six people or more
Light for reading, relaxing, entertaining, ambience
Place for TV, artwork, books, knick-knacks
Coffee table
Reading chair
Landings or end tables to place coffee/tea, drinks
Sofa large enough to lie on
Storage for books, TV, stereo, CDs, tapes, speakers
Storage for media/communication center, wireless
printer
Room for dog bed

Living Room Furniture Rose Wants to Keep and Use

Black chest to hold sweaters, shawls, etc.
Bertoia chair

Media/Music stuff/receiver, DVD, CD, TV

Side tables: Chinese black cart, Chinese porcelain barrel

Ikea bookshelf

Gold framed mirror

Geisha collage piece

Wicker magazine holder

Larry's Cambodian fabric art

Photos

Altar Kwan Yin figurine and incense pot

Wooden monk

Wicker magazine holder

Gourd pottery

CD storage racks

Other Needs and Desires

Media Center for music, TV and communication devices

Smart TV, wireless printer, laptop, receiver, turntable, DVD/CD, etc. in a low console unit. Roll-out shelves in console to hold printer and office supplies

Placement possibly on northeast wall

Pull-down shades

Sofabed against southwest wall

Built-in shelves under kitchen counter in living room to house CDs and books

Two reading lamps

Wireless speakers

Expandable table that starts out small and flips open at sides

Hinged table top to act as prep table when needed or extra table

Kitchen and Dining Area

Most important part of the house because Rose and
Larry likes to cook and entertain

General Needs

Room to eat and entertain 2–12 guests
Space for two cooks to work without killing each other
Food preparation counter space
Light for visual and emotional needs
Storage space for large appliances and tools
Storage space for plates, glasses, silverware, tablecloths,
    dishtowels, pans
Storage space for dry dog food
Counter space for cooking tools
Pantry for dry foods
Area for cleaning supplies
Spice cabinet and tea cabinet
Place to put meds and vitamins
Place for telephone/message center
Knobs or handles to accommodate arthritis
Cabinet pull-out shelves to accommodate difficulties
    lifting heavy pans, appliances
Towel racks

Supplies and Equipment
Placement and Storage for the Following Items

Rubber mats to stand on while preparing meals
Nesting mixing bowls
Mixing bowls – stainless steel – large and extra large

Standard size and mini food processor

Blender

Standing mixer

Toaster

Microwave

Soup bowls

Salad/dessert plates

Storage container for dry dog food

Dinner plates

Mugs for every day as well as company

Water/wine glasses

Serving plates and platters

Electric kettle

Tea pot

Coffee urn; one for six cups, one for 24 cups

Pitchers for holding cooking utensils

(4) Cookie sheets

(3) Pie pans

(3) 13 × 9 (.33 meters × .23 meters) pans

(2) Baking racks

(4) Cutting boards

Knives and sharpener

Cooking tools/spoons, tongs, flippers,

Measuring cups/spoons

Silverware

Towels, aprons, potholders

Trivets

Vases

Water pitchers

Brita container

Condiments

Stock pots

Spices; various jars, bags of dried peppers

Grains; rice, pasta

Candles

Pots, pans, casserole-type pans

Dining/Kitchen Area Placement and Storage

Expandable dining table

Dining chairs

Tablecloths

Candlesticks

Cloth napkins

Placemats

Baking pans on shelf under butcher block

Cutting boards vertically placed in lower cabinet next
to large

Bathroom

Activities: bath, shower, toileting, make-up grooming.
We need place to store bath supplies, make-up,
medicinal needs

General Needs

A place for serenity

Easily manipulated handles and feature with hose
feature

Good lighting for make-up

Good sized mirror

Hooks for robe, bath towels, face and hand towels

Location of towel rack so they get good ventilation

Good light for visual and emotional needs

Towels

Toiletry (soap, toothpaste, shampoos, conditioner,
ointments, first aid, aspirin, make-up, skin cream,
things like dental stuff, Q-tips, cotton balls)

Three-tiered shelf

Electric toothbrushes

Lotions

Bathroom Desires

Shelving for toiletry

Under-sink shelving

Full-length mirror

Hooks for towels next to shower

Drying arrangement for towels such as double rack, one
above the other

Clothes hamper

Projected Future Needs

Hand grips in shower for additional support

I will buy desired furnishings, etc. in phases over time by
prioritizing need and affordability

Aesthetics, Desires, Emotional Satisfaction

This is what Rose dreams about in terms of items, colors, shapes
and textures in their house:

A sectional

A Moroccan red wall

A turmeric yellow Moroccan theme wall in kitchen

A kitchen/dining area that feels exciting and energizing

A peaceful serene bedroom

Luxurious bedding

LIST OF BOXES

INDEX

transition: color 126; space to space 142–4,
147–50, 322
transparency 92, 100–1
Treve Johnson Photography 22, 24
Tucker, L. M. 176, 186
Turcznski, K. 23, 25–8, 147, 151–9, 271

unity: principle of design 83, 88, 91, 125,
165, 317
universal, accessible, aging in place, and healthy
environment design 5, 20–1, 24, 46, 54–5, 62,
283, 310, 349, 351; see case studies

variables in lighting 107–8, 116–8
values: color 83, 120–3, 125–6; human 3, 11,
13–4, 17, 19, 34, 37, 98, 214, 250, 277,
284–5; lighting 116–9; see case studies;
programming worksheets
variety: principle of design 14, 27, 38, 81, 83, 85,
88–9, 90, 101–3, 110–1, 120–1, 125–6, 144,
149, 191, 198, 228, 285, 316–7

Viani, L. O. 21, 30
view: global 17, 77, 250
visual perception 13, 15–6
visual impression 17
Visser Architects 61
visual characteristics: impression 15, 17,
perception; 13, 15–6

wabi-sabi 246–7
websites, craigslist, eBay,
Freecycle 245
WEISBACH architecture | design xix, 16,
45, 93, 171, 200, 270
WELL Building Institute 21
WELL Building Standard 21, 119
Wilde Construction 61
Wilson, E. O. 87, 105, 164, 186
Worksheets see programming worksheets

Zimmerman, C. xvii, 21–9
Zimmerman, J. xvii, 21–9